DUNBAR

MINING THE SURFACES

Edward Lucie-Smith

1997 NEW ORLEANS MUSEUM OF ART

2,000 copies of this catalogue were published in conjunction with the exhibition DUNBAR, MINING THE SURFACES organized by the New Orleans Museum of Art.

November 15, 1997 - January 7, 1998

ISBN 0-89494-061-9

Designed by: Ed Biggs Design, New Orleans, Louisiana
Printed by: Harvey Press, New Orleans, Louisiana
Cover: Detail of *Untitled,* 1996

Table of Contents

Lenders

Alexandria Museum of Art

Mr. and Mrs. Howard Barnett

Dr. and Mrs. John C. Bowen, III

Mr. and Mrs. Joseph Canizaro

Jeanne Cimino and Marc Dobriner

Mr. and Mrs. Arthur Q. Davis

Carol and Bill Deasy

George B. Dunbar

Entergy Corporation

Mr. and Mrs. Robert J. Fabacher

Dr. and Mrs. John Fraiche

Galerie Simonne Stern

Mr. and Mrs. Charles F. Gay, Jr.

Mr. and Mrs. Charles Goodyear, IV

Mr. and Mrs. George W. Healy, IV

James Reid Holden

Leon Irwin, III

Donna Perret and Richard Johnson

Kay and Robert Kerrigan

Mr. and Mrs. H. Merritt Lane, Jr.

Dr. H. Russell Albright and Lee H. Ledbetter

Anne and King Milling

Biff and Barbara Motley

James A. Mounger

Mr. and Mrs. O. Miles Pollard, Jr.

Anne Pratt

Mrs. James W. Reily, Jr.

Mr. and Mrs. William G. Richards

Françoise B. Richardson

Dr. Kenneth Saer, Jr.

Dr. Mit Seiler

Tulane University School of Law

Mrs. Edmund Vales

Four Anonymous Lenders

Preface and Acknowledgments

Gold, universally prized for its precious rarity and mythic beauty, has been utilized by artists since the dawn of civilization, in ancient Egypt, China, India and the Americas. Later in Europe on Byzantine icons and Italian trecento paintings, gold leaf was used as the background to symbolize the realm of Heaven. In Latin America after the Conquest, the abundance of gold permitted the Spanish to lavishly decorate the interior of their new churches, where nearly every surface sparkled with gold leaf.

Considering this rich, world tradition of working in gold, it is surprising that George Dunbar is nearly unique among contemporary artists to extensively employ gold and other metal leaf to create a substantial body of two- and three-dimensional work. The Euclidean geometric patterns in Dunbar's paintings — sometimes minimal, more recently robustly baroque — are drawn and incised under and over layers of light-reflecting metal leaf. The results are works which are simultaneously austere and sumptuous. The New Orleans Museum of Art is proud to present this nearly forty-year survey of George Dunbar's art, with an emphasis on his metal leaf creations.

Many individuals have generously cooperated with the Museum in organizing the exhibition. I am happy to again thank Edward Lucie-Smith for serving as the guest curator of one of our exhibitions. His incredibly broad knowledge of contemporary art gives him the perspective and insight to write the catalog essay on Dunbar's art. On the artist's studio staff, we were ably assisted by Blake Boyd and Jane Whitty. The artist has long been represented by Galerie Simonne Stern, where the director Donna Perret and her staff helped to locate and have photographed works in the exhibition. The fine photographs were taken by Glade Bilby and this handsome publication was designed by Ed Biggs. At the Museum, the exhibition details were coordinated first by Sharon Stearns, until recently Curator of Paintings, and then by Ann Meehan, Curator of Education, working with Paul Tarver, Registrar, and Pat Pecoraro, Curator of Exhibitions.

Finally I extend the Museum's special appreciation to the many lenders who so graciously agreed to part with their Dunbar paintings and sculptures so that a much larger audience could enjoy them. The lenders' generosity is a testament of their devotion to George Dunbar and their love of his beautiful and elegant art.

E. John Bullard

Director

GEORGE DUNBAR

by Edward Lucie-Smith

George Dunbar occupies a unique position in the recent history of the visual arts in New Orleans. On the one hand he is, as he himself declares, "a local yokel," and on the other he is a maker of work with universal implications. The story of his career is full of resonances for students of the contemporary American cultural scene.

Though New Orleans and its environs have now become favored places of residence for artists, few of these are as intimately linked to this area of Louisiana as he is. His mother's family were sugar planters in an area very close to the city; his father was a member of the oldest law firm in the city. He and his brother were both meant to follow their father's footsteps and pursue legal careers — "but early on I made a wise decision not to become a lawyer." Did the positive decision to become an artist follow immediately on the negative one not to follow his father's footsteps? Dunbar is not sure that it did, though certain early influences were at work: "One thing that was a factor was that my mother took me with her to New York every year." Her way of disposing of him when it looked as if he might be underfoot was to take him to the Metropolitan Museum of Art. "I was left there and told that I was very fortunate to be there for two hours alone. That forced me to look at things — it turned out to be a very worthwhile experience."

The decision to become an artist followed a period in the service. Unlike the wars which followed it in the second half of the twentieth century, World War II was a popular cause with young Americans. George Dunbar joined the Navy straight out of high school and worked as a salvage diver for two years. When he came out, it was time to go to university. Since his family was a prosperous one, this is the course he would have followed anyway. But what his period in the service did was to free him from any obligation to follow his parents' wishes in his choice of what course of studies he followed, since he now had access to the benefits conferred by the GI Bill. Sure now of the path he wanted to pursue, Dunbar elected to study art.

Another aspect of his freedom of choice was that he was at liberty to choose not only his course of study but also the institution at which he enrolled. As he saw it, the choice lay between Cranbrook Academy of Art (Bloomfield Hills, Michigan) and Tyler School of Art at Temple University in Philadelphia — then the two most prestigious art schools in the coun-

The Background

try. His choice fell on Tyler "because of the location — I could see art shows on the weekend in New York."

At this point it is worth recalling, however briefly, what the American art world was like at that period: the late 1940s and early 1950s. The Abstract Expressionist style, born in the earlier years of the 1940s, had now become a dominant force. The leadership of American painting was becoming recognized worldwide, and New York was in the process of replacing Paris as the focus of artistic innovation. Let me cite a few key dates: In 1943 Arshile Gorky painted his *Garden in Sochi* series, and Jackson Pollock had his first solo exhibition at Peggy Guggenheim's Art of this Century Gallery. In 1947 Pollock began making his "drip" paintings, and in the following year Barnett Newman started making color field paintings. In 1949 Robert Motherwell began painting his *Elegies to the Spanish Republic*. In 1951 The Museum of Modern Art in New York held its survey exhibition *Abstract Painting and Sculpture in America*, now generally recognized as an official consecration of the new school. In 1952 the influential New York critic Harold Rosenberg coined the term 'Action Painting,' which was to gain wide currency among his fellow critics, among artists, and with the general public.

George Dunbar graduated from Tyler in 1951 with a degree in painting, and these were the influences to which he was exposed. He names Willem de Kooning as one of his chief influences at this time, though as much for the traditional as for the revolutionary aspect of his work: "I could see that de Kooning continued to draw as he painted — he allowed the sculptural aspects of drawing to become part of his painting." Other influences were "Kline, maybe Motherwell, maybe Rothko a little bit. I was an Action Painter."

The only one of these major figures he knew personally was Franz Kline. They even exhibited together in Philadelphia on one occasion. Dunbar recalls a useful lesson gained from the calligraphy Kline painted on pages torn from telephone books: "He realized that if you have to go back and rework an area, you lose the vigor. If you're dealing with a surface you can't correct that surface. It has to be there."

There was another and very important aspect of Tyler, however, which had nothing to do with its propinquity to New York. This was the strong emphasis which its system of teaching placed on the technical tradition: "You had to learn to grind your own paints. You had to learn various processes such as underpainting and things of that kind — traditional methods of oil painting." Anyone who encounters George Dunbar's work today will immediately recognize that, while his methods are now seldom 'traditional' in the narrow sense sometimes given to that term, he nevertheless has an enormous respect for refinements of technical skill — he is unashamedly a virtuoso, at a time when virtuosity has become suspect. No one confronted with an example of his work would venture to utter the now time-hallowed put-down: "A child of ten could do it."

After leaving Tyler, George Dunbar travelled in Europe for a year, spending some time in Paris working in another traditional setting, La Grande Chaumiere, one of several long-established "free" (in the sense of not being linked to the French official system) academies where aspiring artists, among them many foreigners, came to draw and paint.

The thing which drew him back to New Orleans was his mother's ill-health. "I hadn't planned to go back, but when I did it grabbed me — there was something I realized I really missed about the city." The problem which immediately confronted him, however, was that which confronts all young artists: that of how to make a living. In the 1950s, New Orleans, a relatively small city by American standards, had only a very rudimentary infrastructure for the support of contemporary art. Dunbar had his first exhibition in the city in 1955 at the 331 Gallery, which was the offshoot of what was essentially an interior decorating business. He taught at a school adjacent to this gallery and also conducted workshops at the Tulane University School of Architecture, but it soon became clear to him that this was no way to make a living or for that matter to build a career.

Finding a solution to these problems took him in two apparently quite different directions. The 1950s were a crucial moment in the actual physical development of the city. Hitherto compact, confined between the Mississippi River and Lake Pontchartrain, it was just beginning, like many other American communities, to burst its boundaries, influenced both by population growth and by the availability of the automobile. Dunbar decided that he wanted to develop real estate in the suburbs, preferably on sites overlooking water which is such an important physical and psychological element of local traditions. Much of the hinterland north of New Orleans was successfully reshaped by him — reshaped, often, in an extremely literal sense, since he made bayous and canals where none had existed previously. The double life he led — working as a real estate developer by day, and as an artist in the evening and at night — was, he now admits, sometimes unduly stressful. Not only did he spend "many all-night sessions" working at his art, but the demands of his day job were themselves often heavy. "You take your business problems home with you, and sometimes it interferes with the time you use for making art, so there were periods when [being a real estate developer] was a diversion." On the other hand, there were aesthetic compensations even in his business activities. "I did a lot of earth-moving, a lot of digging of canals and things of this kind, and I got a lot of satisfaction out of that. There was some similarity to working in a medium that no one else had worked with in art." Perhaps, if he had belonged to a slightly younger generation, Dunbar might have thrown in his lot with the Land Artists of the late 1960s and early 1970s — men like Robert Smithson and Michael Heizer.

He was also touched by the attitudes towards his parallel activity as an artist which he found among the people who worked with him on his real estate development projects. "People respected the fact that you did it — they tried not to burden your time. There was respect for someone who was doing something different. Possibly they didn't understand what I was doing, but they recognized I was serious about it."

Another aspect of that seriousness was his determination not only to find a way of making art, but of presenting it professionally. The response by Dunbar and five fellow artists was the creation, in the mid-1950s, of the Orleans Gallery, the first artists' co-operative gallery in New Orleans, and almost certainly the first in the whole of the American South. The Orleans Gallery is now generally acknowledged as the kernel from which the whole of the present vigorous contemporary art scene in New Orleans was to sprout. It must nevertheless be added that the growth of contemporary art in the city might not have been so rapid without the support of the New Orleans Museum of Art, then called the Issac Delgado Museum of Art. Dunbar was given a solo exhibition there in August 1964. The present show, held just over thirty-three years later, is the successor to that enterprise.

The work displayed in 1964 could be broadly described as "action paintings" — this, indeed, is the term the artist himself still uses for them. The present selection looks very unlike most peoples' notion of action painting or any form of Abstract Expressionism. The first thing to emphasize, therefore, is that this is a deliberately incomplete view of George Dunbar's achievement, though it does feature techniques and types of imagery for which he is now well-known. In addition to things which can broadly speaking be described as paintings, there are a number of fully three-dimensional objects. What most of the paintings and objects have in common is their employment of metal leaf. Three metals are involved — gold, platinum and palladium — but the gold comes in a number of different hues according to the alloy. Stylistically the works fall into two groups. There are some which make use of compass-drawn designs, others which are freer and more baroque. The three-dimensional pieces fall almost entirely into the second category.

George Dunbar first began to use metal leaf in the 1960s.* At this time he was making numerous trips to Mexico, because his wife liked it. Among the places he visited were Mexico City, Cuernavaca and Cozumel. While he was not attracted to Mexican contemporary art, which to his eye had too close a resemblance to that of the American Regionalists — Thomas Hart Benton and others (the ruling hegemony Abstract Expressionism had overthrown) — he did gradually become fascinated with the gilded surfaces he saw in Mexican churches. He was attracted not to historical associations but to the integral yet mysteriously reflective surface. Dunbar was already accustomed to making collages, but there was something about the nature of collage that troubled him. "I always objected when one surface stood away from the picture plane so to speak. The problem was to incorporate gold leaf into painting without its acquiring a decorative aspect that I did not want."

The application of gold leaf to a surface imposes its own rules. It is applied to a very fine, very smooth clay surface using rabbit-skin glue. That is, in a broad sense, it is a painstaking, artisanal technique related to the traditional oil painting techniques which Dunbar had mastered during his student years at Tyler. What he now wanted to do was to find some way of reconciling this method of working with the Abstract Expressionist ethos which was still important to him. To begin with, he was content to follow the rules the material seemed to lay down for itself. Early examples emphasize the square shapes of the gold leaf, which is supplied in this form in what is appropriately known as a "book."

Dunbar says that, at this stage, he was still ignorant of some of the problems — the adverse impact of moisture, the way some of the less high-carat leaf tended to tarnish, as indeed did the silver leaf with which he occasionally experimented. At the same time, he was already beginning to feed in to the work ideas and techniques suggested by previous, more orthodox forms of artistic activity. For example, at one time he had made string drawings

— "take a string, dip it in ink, drag it over the canvas." He wanted to find a technique with the same spontaneity. He found, for example, that the metal leaf surfaces were even less susceptible to being reworked than rapid drawings of the type Franz Kline had made. Since he had been making some prints, he decided to see how the new surface would respond to engraving. But here again problems arose. It was very difficult to use dry-point techniques freehand. In addition, the lines made by the engraving tool were not sufficiently visible at a distance. The solutions were complex — to use compass-drawn lines, to use a series of very fine lines close together, and to use numerous layers of clay in different colors. Though Dunbar does not make the comparison, there is an affinity here with certain aspects of traditional Japanese lacquer technique, which also discovers spontaneous effects within a very laborious and painstaking technical framework.

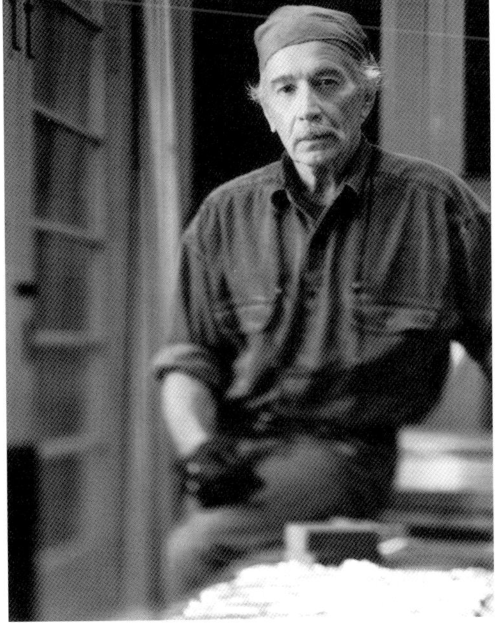

Dunbar also perceived that the fine clay to which the leaf was applied was itself "a very sensual material," and this encouraged him to build it up, often using rags as a foundation, then modeling paste shaped with a spatula, before applying the final coating of metal leaf. Using a spatula to draw into the still-wet surface of the modeling paste seemed to him to offer a method equivalent to the string drawings which he had once produced — something just as free and spontaneous. In addition, as he notes, there was "a natural evolution from the modeled pieces to things which were [fully] three-dimensional."

Though the flat, engraved works sometimes make use of recognizable symbols, such as a heart, one of the striking differences between them and the modeled works is that the latter tend to be markedly more figurative. In particular, many of the modeled works, both those in relief and those fully in the round, offer allusions to the female body. The kind of body Dunbar favors is very much like that employed by de Kooning in his celebrated ***Women*** paintings — broad-hipped and deep-breasted. So here, too, there is a connection with the Abstract Expressionism Dunbar has never wholly abandoned, though he has, over the years, transformed it until its presence becomes almost unrecognizable.

If one looks at ways of trying to bring the two aspects of the metal leaf works together intellectually, so that they coalesce into a whole, I think it can be done through metaphor, and through reference to the broad outline of Dunbar's biography which has been given above. The compass-drawn works, it seems to me, can be thought of as being maps, or architectural plans, or better still as plans for gardens. Digging into their clay surfaces, deliberately distressing them through sanding (sometimes even by firing shotgun shells at them), Dunbar was doing a version of some of the things he did when reshaping the environs of New Orleans. The figurative works supply the more specifically human element, and transfer the idea of fecundity (so important to the physical climate of Louisiana) to a different plane.

One of the fascinating things about metal leaf is that, while it is obviously sensual and sumptuous — something that offers physical delight in a very direct, uninhibited way — it can also be withdrawn and ambiguous. For example, as the spectator changes position in relation to some of the works shown here, more particularly the flat ones, various aspects of the overall design appear, then disappear, according to the angle of view and how the light itself strikes the picture plane. These are not works from which one can extract their fullest meaning by treating them in a passive way. They demand the viewer's cooperation. It is not too much to say that we are invited to enter into a kind of dance. I think they will delight visitors to the exhibition just as they delight me. Quite apart from that, they represent one of the most distinguished bodies of visual work to have been produced in New Orleans during the past few decades.

Author's Note: All material in quotation marks is taken from tape-recorded interviews between the author and George Dunbar.

**According to his own account - some works in this medium currently carry indeterminate dates in the 1950s.*

Biographical Chronology

Selected Exhibitions, Solo:

Galerie Simonne Stern,
New Orleans, LA,
Oct. 4-28, 1997

Galerie Simonne Stern,
New Orleans, LA,
Nov. 5-30,1994

Cultural Arts Center,
Slidell, LA,
April 8-28, 1994 - Retrospective

Galerie Simonne Stern,
New Orleans, LA,
Nov. 2-Dec. 2, 1992

Imperial Calcasieu Museum,
Lake Charles, LA,
Sept. 20-Oct. 25, 1992

Galerie Nadeau,
Philadelphia, PA,
March 23-April 5, 1991

Galerie Simonne Stern,
New Orleans, LA,
Jan. 5-Feb. 5, 1991

St. Tammany Art Association,
Covington, LA,
Jan. 8-29, 1989

Galerie Simonne Stern,
New Orleans, LA,
Nov. 5-30, 1988

Galerie Simonne Stern,
New Orleans, LA,
May 9-27, 1987

Heath Gallery,
Atlanta, GA,
Sept. 7-Oct. 5, 1985

Galerie Simonne Stern,
New Orleans, LA,
Dec. 8, 1984-Jan. 3, 1985

Galerie Simonne Stern,
New Orleans, LA,
April 9-27, 1983

Galerie Simonne Stern,
New Orleans, LA,
Nov. 15-Dec. 4, 1980

Galerie Simonne Stern,
New Orleans, LA,
Nov. 11-30, 1978

Galerie Simonne Stern,
New Orleans, LA,
May 8-27, 1976

Galerie Simonne Stern,
New Orleans, LA,
Nov. 13-30, 1974

Heath Gallery,
Atlanta, GA,
April 9-30, 1974

Galerie Simonne Stern,
New Orleans, LA,
Feb. 11-24, 1973

Orleans Gallery,
New Orleans, LA,
Nov. 22-Dec. 12, 1970

Orleans Gallery,
New Orleans, LA,
April 13-26, 1969

Orleans Gallery,
New Orleans, LA,
Jan. 13-Feb. 1, 1968

Orleans Gallery,
New Orleans, LA,
April 11-25, 1965

Delgado Museum (New
Orleans Museum of Art),
New Orleans, LA,
Aug. 2-13, 1964

Orleans Gallery,
New Orleans, LA,
Jan. 13-19, 1963

Orleans Gallery,
New Orleans, LA, 1960

Parma Gallery,
New York, NY, 1958

Orleans Gallery,
New Orleans, LA, 1957

Parma Gallery,
New York, NY, 1956

331 Gallery,
New Orleans, LA, 1955

Dubin-Luch Gallery,
Philadelphia, PA, 1955

Dubin-Luch Gallery,
Philadelphia, PA, 1953

Selected Exhibitions, Group:

St. Tammany Art Assn.,
Covington, LA

"Drawing Invitational,"
Galerie Simonne Stern,
New Orleans, LA

Delfina Studio Trust, London,
"Louisiana Story," curated by
Edward Lucie-Smith

University of New Orleans,
Fine Arts Gallery,
New Orleans, LA

Rose Museum, Brandeis
University, Waltham, MA

Temple University,
Philadelphia, PA

New Orleans Museum of Art,
New Orleans, LA

Contemporary Arts Center,
New Orleans, LA

Riverside Museum,
New York City, NY

Sea Island Museum,
Sea Island, GA

Bressler Gallery,
Milwaukee, WI

Newcomb Gallery,
Tulane University,
New Orleans, LA

Denver Museum,
Denver, CO

Touring Exhibitions:

Vienna, Austria; Hong Kong,
BCC; Manila, Philippine Island;
Sidney, Australia

Birmingham Museum of Art,
Birmingham, AL

1968 Volkfest, West Germany

Louisiana Art Commission,
Baton Rouge, LA

Pensacola Art Center,
Pensacola, FL

State Capital,
Baton Rouge, LA

Historic New Orleans
Collection, New Orleans, LA

Louisiana World Exposition,
New Orleans, LA

South American Touring
Exhibition

Teaching Experience:

Tulane University, School of
Architecture, New Orleans, LA

331 Art School,
New Orleans, LA

Selected Honors:

Contemporary Arts Center,
New Orleans, LA,
Silver Circle Artist

Tyler School of Fine Arts,
Philadelphia, PA, First Prize,
Painting

New Orleans Museum of Art,
New Orleans, LA,
First Prize, Painting

Rose Museum, Brandeis
University, Waltham, MA,
Purchase Prize

New Orleans Museum of Art, New Orleans, LA, Award Winner- Southeastern Texas Exhibition

1974 Louisiana Bicentennial Exhibition - 2 Purchase Prizes

Selected Articles and Publications:

John Kemp, Review, *The Times Picayune*, April 21, 1994

Ted Calas, *Lagniappe*, November 27. 1992

Roger Green, Review, *The Times Picayune*, January 3, 1991

Ted Calas, *New Orleans Art Review*, January, 1991

Benson & Hedges, advertisement, 1991

Lew Thomas and Tom Dolan, *Louisiana Artists' Pages*, Contemporary Arts Center, Feb. 25, 1989

Myrna Bridgeman, Review, *The Daily Sentry News*, October 2, 1988

John Kemp, Review, *The Times Picayune*, January 8, 1988

Louisiana Life Magazine, January/February 1988

Louisiana Life Magazine, November/December 1987, featured

Roger Green, Review, *The Times Picayune*, May 22, 1987

Jason Berry, Review, *New Orleans Magazine*, April 1985

Art News, 1984

Ted Calas, *New Orleans Art Review Magazine*, May 1983

The Historic New Orleans Collection, 1982

Ted Calas, *Abstraction in Louisiana*, Contemporary Arts Center, October 4-26, 1980

Figaro, Review, November 22, 1978

Alberta Collier, Review, *The Times Picayune*, May 6,1976

The Atlanta Journal, April 18, 1974

Alberta Collier, Review, *The Times Picayune*, February 11, 1973

Figaro, February 24, 1973

Vieux Carre Courier, Review, February 1973

Accolade, November 1972, feature

Alberta Collier, Review, *The Times Picayune*, January 25, 1968

La Revue Moderne, Paris, France, May 1, 1967, feature

Art in America, "New Talent USA," Al Lansford, featured, February 1955

Walter Baum, Review, *Inquirer*, November 1953

Art News, November 1953

Education:

Tyler School of Art, Temple University, Philadelphia, PA, B.F.A. in Painting, 1951

Grande Chaumiere, Paris, France, 1953

Selected Public Collections:

Tulane University, Law School, New Orleans, LA

Alexandria Museum of Art, Alexandria, LA

Arts Council of New Orleans

North Carolina Museum of Art, Raleigh, NC

Monroe, Lemann, Attorneys, New Orleans, LA

New Orleans Museum of Art

Pan American Life Corporation, New Orleans, LA

Lenfant's Restaurant, New Orleans, LA

City National Bank, Baton Rouge, LA

Jones Walker, et al, Attorneys, New Orleans, LA

Westminister City Properties, The Equitable Center, 1615 Poydras Street, New Orleans, LA

Bank of New Orleans

Texaco Center (Lobby), New Orleans, LA

Phelps, Dunbar, Marks, Claverie and Simms, Attorneys, New Orleans, LA

First National Bank of Commerce, Covington, LA

L L & E Tower (Lobby), New Orleans, LA

Lykes Steamship Co., New Orleans, LA

Jefferson Guaranty Bank (Lobby), New Orleans, LA

One River Place (Lobby), New Orleans, LA

Commerce Bank (Lobby), St. Louis, MO

Entergy Corp., Washington, D.C.

Rose Museum, Brandeis University, Waltham, MA

Lambert and Nelson, Attorneys, New Orleans, LA

George Dunbar is represented by:

New Orleans:
Galerie Simonne Stern,
518 Julia Street,
New Orleans, LA

Atlanta:
Heath Gallery,
416 East Paces Ferry Road,
Atlanta, GA

Chicago:
Neville-Sargent Gallery,
410 N. Milwaukee Ave.,
Libertyville, IL

Works In The Exhibition

Untitled, 1950
Gold over clay
49 x 49 inches
Collection of
Mrs. James W. Reily, Jr.

Untitled, 1950
Gold over clay
$15^1/_2$ x $21^1/_2$ inches
Collection of Mr. and Mrs.
William G. Richards

◗ *Red M,* 1959
Acrylic and paper collage
50 x 47 inches
Collection of the Artist

Untitled, 1961
Red and blue acrylic and
collage
12 x 14 inches
Collection of the Artist

Untitled, 1961
Red and blue acrylic and
collage
16 x 49 inches
Collection of the Artist

Untitled, 1962
24k gold leaf, modeling
paste and clay
49 x $41^1/_2$ inches
Collection of Mr. and Mrs.
Arthur Q. Davis

◗ *Untitled,* 1965
Gold and silver leaf over clay
15 x 31 inches
Anonymous

Untitled, 1966
Green, black and white
paper collage and stone
$18^1/_8$ x $19^5/_8$ inches
Collection of Mrs. Edmund
Vales

◗ *Untitled,* 1967
Silver leaf over clay
23 x $24^3/_4$ inches
Collection of Mr. and Mrs.
William G. Richards

Circles and Squares, 1970
White gold
25 x 25 inches
Collection of Anne Pratt

Untitled, 1970
White gold
$11^3/_4$ x $12^1/_2$ inches
Collection of the Artist

◗ *Untitled,* 1970
White gold
23 x $24^3/_4$ inches
Collection of the Artist

Untitled, 1970
12 and 16k gold
48 x 96 inches
Collection of Mr. and Mrs.
O. Miles Pollard, Jr.

◗ *Untitled,* 1979
Envelope collage
53 x 61 inches
Collection of the Artist

Icebreaker, 1982
Silver leaf over clay
13 x 17 x 4 inches
Collection of Donna Perret
and Richard Johnson

◗ *Untitled,* 1983
Mixed media
9 x 14 x 4 inches
Collection of the Artist

Basil, 1984
Acrylic and collage
48 x 63 inches
Collection of Anne Pratt

Untitled, 1985
Gold leaf
48 x 72 inches
Collection of the Entergy
Corporation

Figure Drawing #2, 1988
Clay on paper
22 x $23^1/_4$ inches
Collection of the Artist

Firebreaker, 1988
Gold leaf and mixed
media
13 x 17 inches
Anonymous

◗ *Las Gordas,* 1988
Egg emulsion
$49^1/_2$ x 62 inches
Anonymous

Untitled, 1988
23k gold over wood
33 x 15 inches
Collection of Mr. and Mrs.
Howard Barnett

Two Ladies, 1988
Egg emulsion
$17^1/_2$ x $21^1/_2$ inches
Collection of Anne Pratt

Untitled, 1989
Moon gold over clay
24 x 32 inches
Collection of Kay and
Robert Kerrigan

◗ *The Queen,* 1990
Clay and dental stone
25 x 25 x 10 inches
Collection of Mr. and Mrs.
Joseph Canizaro

◗ *Untitled,* 1990
Gold leaf over board and
red, blue and black clay
$31^1/_4$ x $25^1/_2$ inches
Collection of Leon Irwin, III

Botheric, 1992
Moon gold over clay
14 x 24 x 13 inches
Collection of the Artist

Cerapton, 1992
Moon and white gold
over clay
25 x 37 inches
Collection of Mr. and Mrs.
H. Merritt Lane, Jr.

◗ *Flight,* 1992
Clay over dental stone
7 x $19^1/_2$ inches
Anonymous

◗ *Frampold,* 1992
24k moon gold over clay
13 x $17^1/_4$ inches
Collection of Françoise B.
Richardson

◗ *Loculus,* 1992
Gold over clay
$35^3/_4$ x $49^1/_4$ inches
Collection of Dr. and Mrs.
John C. Bowen, III

Ostensory, 1992
Clay on paper
21 x $23^1/_2$ inches
Collection of Jeanne
Cimino and Marc Dobriner

◗ *Porpax,* 1992
Moon gold over stone
and clay
$11^3/_4$ x 12 x $5^1/_2$ inches
Collection of the Artist

Pyramid, 1992
Clay and rabbit skin glue
37 x $48^3/_4$ inches
Collection of the New
Orleans Museum of Art

Sintea, 1992
Moon and white gold
over clay
24 x 26 inches
Collection of Dr. Kenneth
Saer, Jr.

Untitled, 1993
Gold leaf over red and
black clay
26 x $28^1/_2$ inches
Collection of Galerie
Simonne Stern

Untitled, 1993
Gold leaf over clay and dental stone
26 x 31 inches
Collection of Mr. and Mrs. Charles Goodyear, IV

◗ *Coin du Lestin II,* 1994
Moon gold over clay
$54\frac{3}{4}$ x $49\frac{1}{4}$ inches
Collection of Anne and King Milling

◗ *Coin du Lestin V,* 1994
Lemon gold and clay
55 x $49\frac{1}{4}$ inches
Collection of Dr. Mit Seiler

Coin du Lestin VI, 1994
Platinum over red, green and white clay
$49\frac{1}{4}$ x $43\frac{1}{8}$ inches
Collection of the Artist

Coin du Lestin IX, 1994
French gold over clay
$39\frac{3}{4}$ x $32\frac{3}{4}$ inches
Collection of James Reid Holden

◗ *Coin du Lestin XIII,* 1994
23k French gold over red, green and black clay
55 x $48\frac{3}{8}$ inches
Collection of James A. Mounger

◗ *Coin du Lestin XV,* 1994
White gold over yellow, white and red clay
55 x $49\frac{1}{4}$ inches
Collection of the Artist

Coin du Lestin XX, 1994
23k and 16k gold over yellow clay
$36\frac{1}{2}$ x $35\frac{1}{2}$ inches
Collection of Mr. and Mrs. George W. Healy, IV

Directions, 1994
23k American gold sand-blasted over clay
38 x 49 inches
Collection of the Alexandria Museum of Art

Flora I, 1994
24k American gold over red, green and black clay
36 x $49\frac{1}{4}$ inches
Anonymous

Flora II, 1994
White gold over clay
$43\frac{1}{8}$ x $49\frac{1}{4}$ inches
Collection of Mr. and Mrs. Charles F. Gay, Jr.

◗ *Coin du Lestin XXIII,* 1995
Gold over black and red clay
55 x $49\frac{1}{4}$ inches
Collection of Mr. and Mrs. Robert J. Fabacher

◗ *Untitled,* 1995
Palladium over red and black clay
$49\frac{1}{4}$ x $81\frac{1}{2}$ inches
Collection of the Tulane University School of Law

◗ *Coin du Lestin XXIV,* 1996
Palladium over blue, white and black clay
43 x 43 inches
Collection of Biff and Barbara Motley

◗ *Coin du Lestin XXV,* 1996
Gold over clay
$56\frac{1}{2}$ x 49 inches
Collection of Dr. H. Russell Albright and Lee H. Ledbetter

◗ *Coin du Lestin XXIX,* 1996
23k gold over red, purple and black clay
$49\frac{1}{2}$ x 42 inches
Collection of Carol and Bill Deasy

◗ *Untitled,* 1996
French gold, lemon gold over green and red clay
$26\frac{1}{4}$ x 33 inches
Collection of the Artist

◗ *Coin du Lestin XXXIII,* 1997
Palladium leaf over red, blue and white clay
$57\frac{1}{4}$ x $49\frac{3}{8}$ inches
Collection of the Artist

◗ *Coin du Lestin XXXIV,* 1997
$23\frac{1}{2}$k red gold leaf over beige, black and purple clay
$49\frac{1}{4}$ x $41\frac{1}{4}$ inches
Anonymous

◗ *Coin du Lestin XXXVI,* 1997
Moon gold and palladium leaf over beige, black and red clay
$49\frac{1}{4}$ x $41\frac{1}{4}$ inches
Anonymous

Flora IV, 1997
Moon gold over clay and board
$49\frac{1}{4}$ x $65\frac{1}{4}$ inches
Collection of Dr. and Mrs. John Fraiche

Untitled, 1997
23k red gold leaf over dark mauve and red clay
96 x 92 inches
Collection of the Artist

Untitled, 1997
Moon gold over dark mauve, red and beige clay
73 x 72 inches
Collection of the Artist

◗ *Untitled,* 1997
23k red gold over red clay
58 x 48 inches
Collection of the Artist

Untitled, 1997
Palladium leaf over blue, white and black clay
$49\frac{3}{8}$ x $41\frac{1}{4}$ inches
Collection of the Artist

Untitled, 1997
French gold and 16k pale gold over green clay
25 x 25 inches
Collection of the Artist

◗ *Untitled,* 1997
Gold leaf and clay over dental stone
51 x 36 x 15 inches
Collection of the Galerie Simonne Stern

◗ *Untitled,* 1997
$23\frac{1}{2}$k red gold, sandblasted
$65\frac{1}{8}$ x $49\frac{1}{4}$ inches
Collection of the Artist

Untitled, 1997
Moon gold over brown, red and black clay
$49\frac{3}{8}$ x $41\frac{1}{4}$ inches
Anonymous

◗ *Works illustrated in the catalogue*

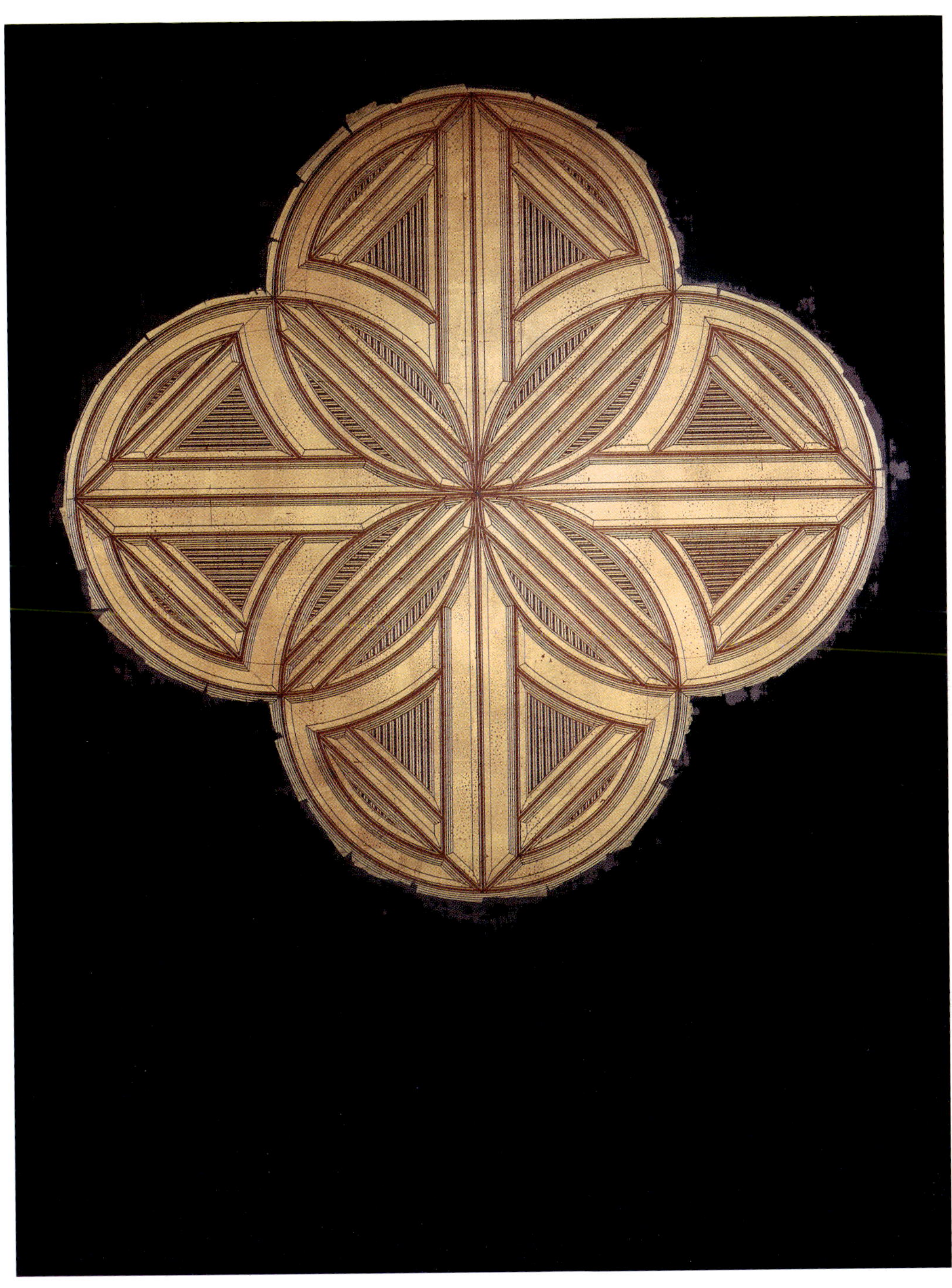

1997
$65\frac{1}{8}$ x $49\frac{1}{4}$ inches
$23\frac{1}{2}$k red gold, sandblasted
Collection of the Artist

Untitled

Untitled

1997
51 x 36 x 15 inches
Gold leaf and clay over dental stone
Collection of Galerie Simonne Stern

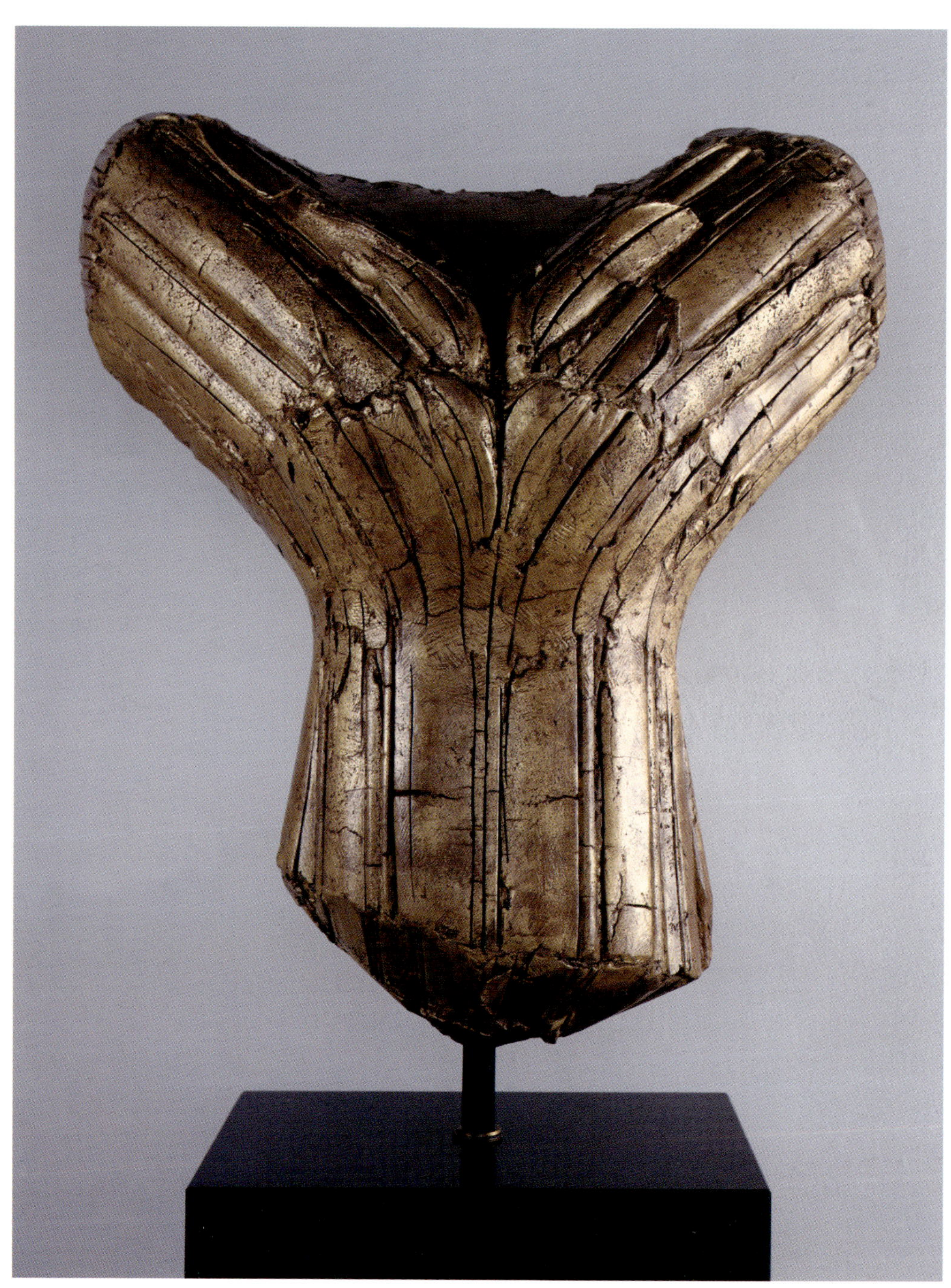

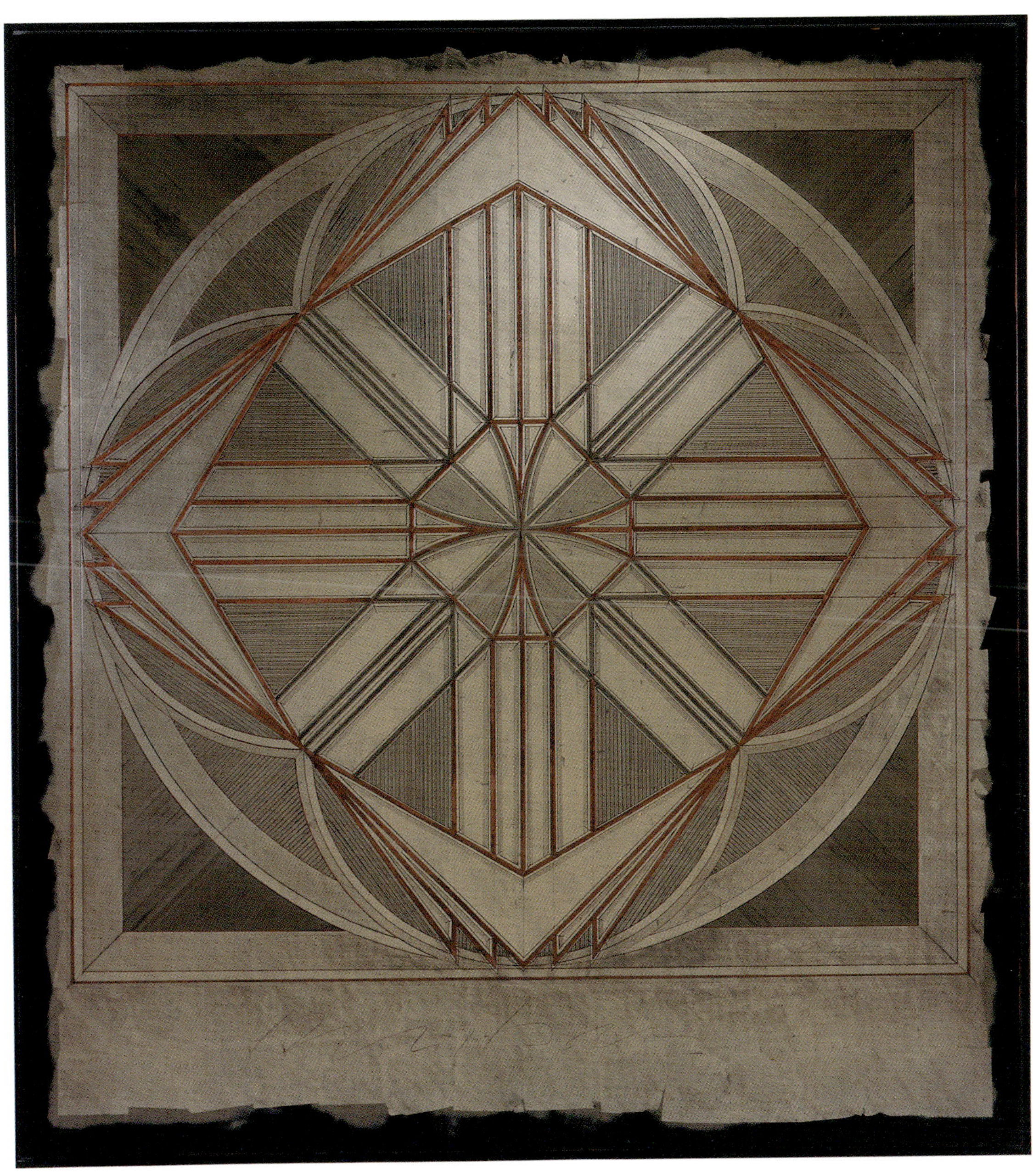

1994
55 x 49 1/4 inches
Lemon gold and clay
Collection of Dr. Mit Seiler

Coin du Lestin V

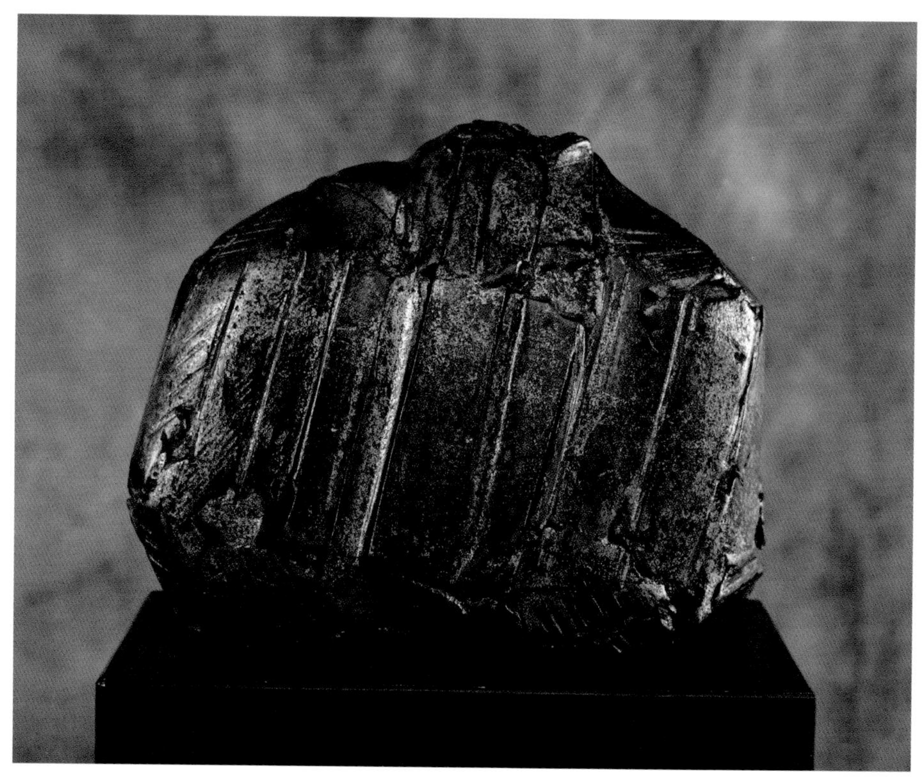

Porpax

1992
11¾ x 12 x 5½ inches
Moon gold over stone and clay
Collection of the Artist

1994
$54^{3}/_{4}$ x $49^{1}/_{2}$ inches
Moon gold over clay
Collection of Anne and King Milling

Coin du Lestin II

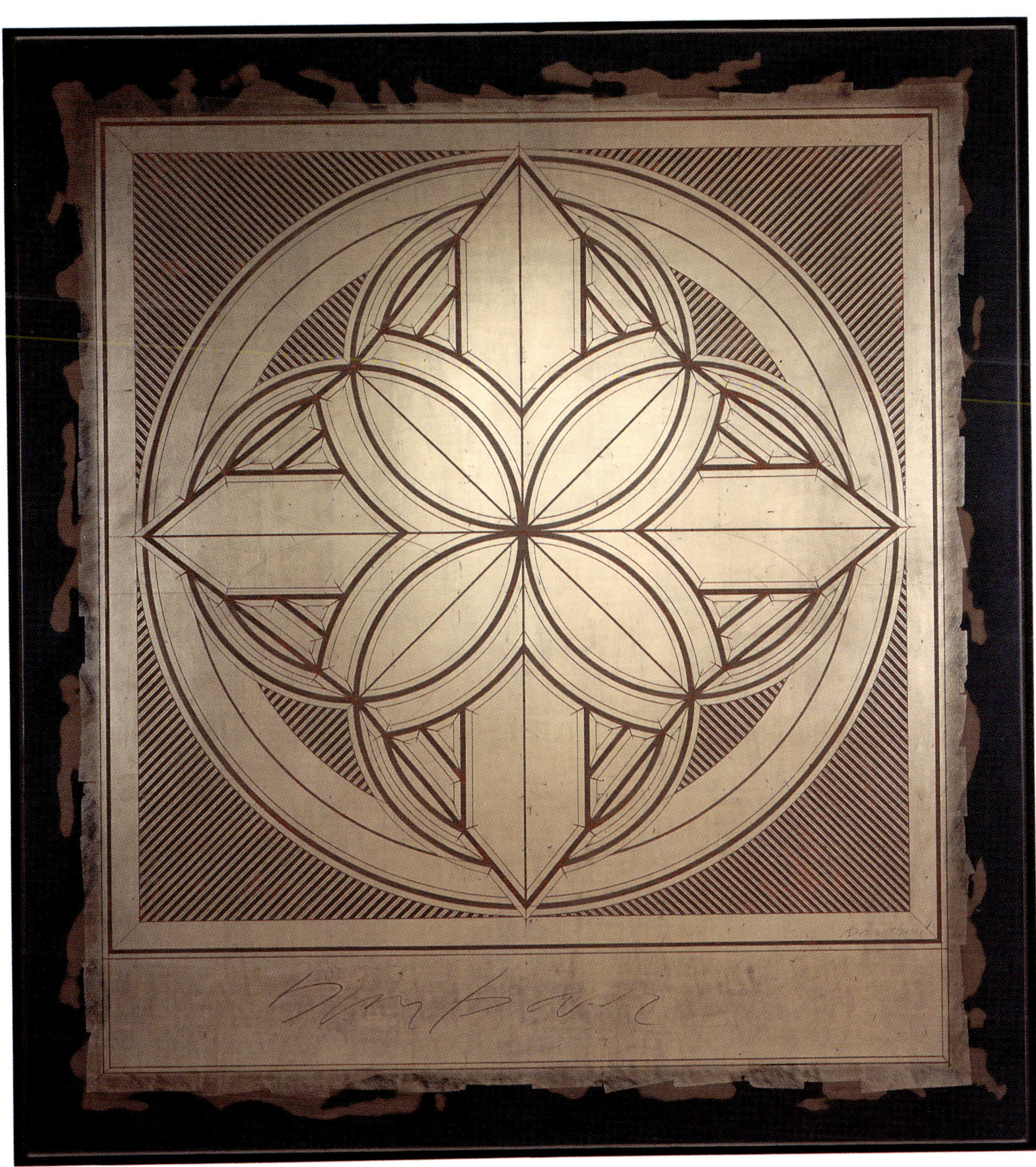

Untitled

1996
$26\frac{1}{4}$ x 33 inches
French gold and lemon gold over green and red clay
Collection of the Artist

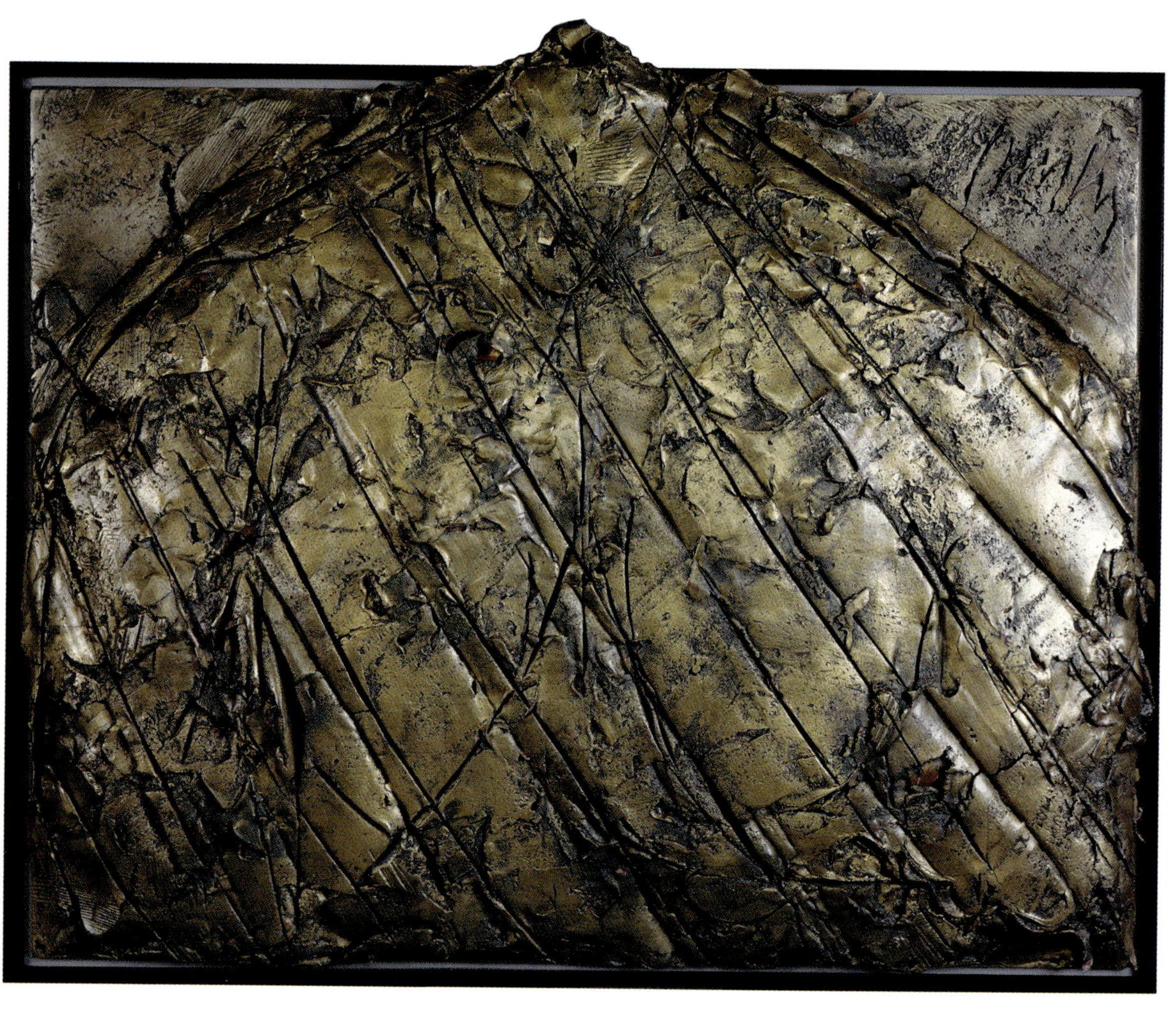

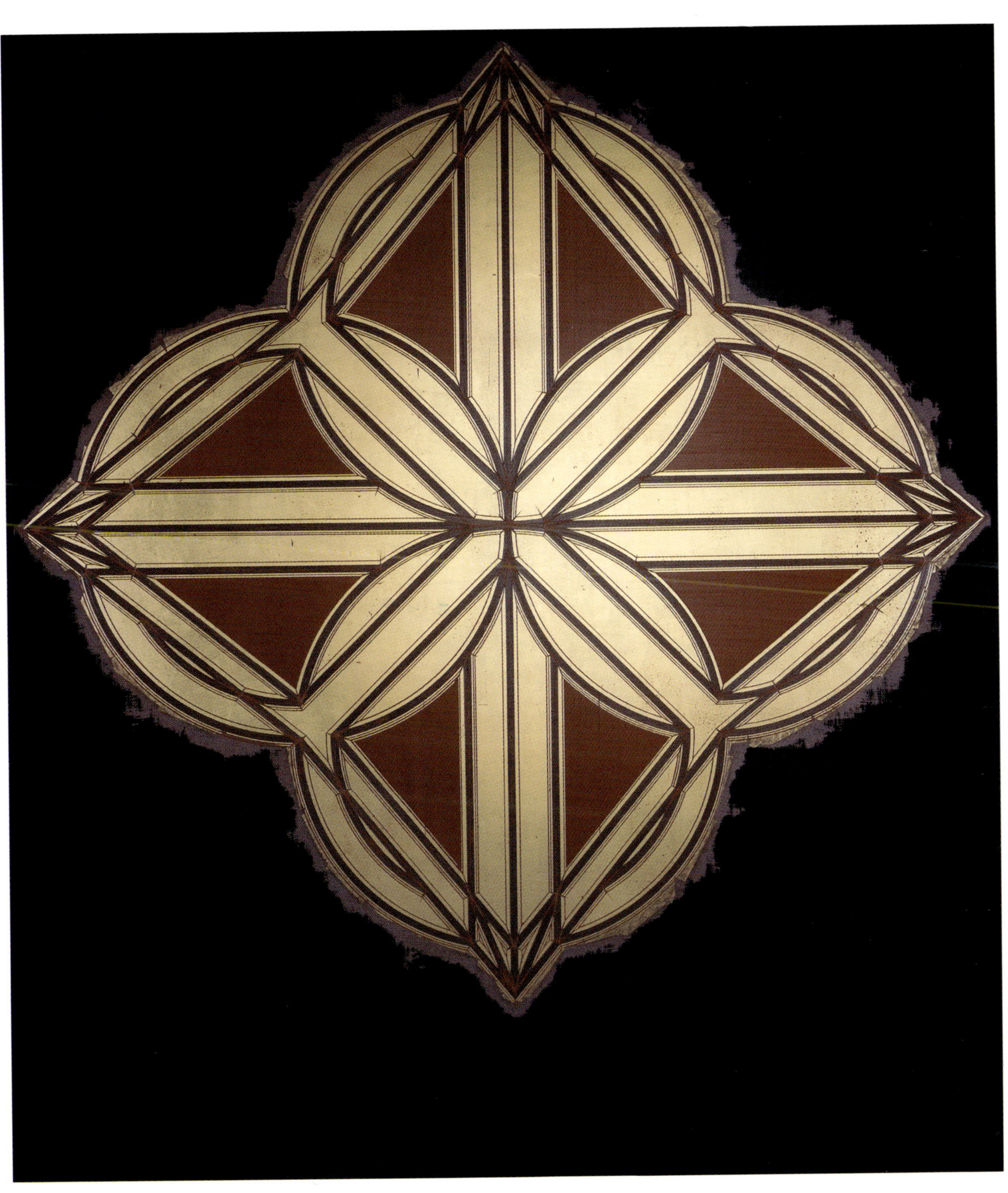

1997
58 x 48 inches
23k red gold over red clay
Collection of the Artist

Untitled

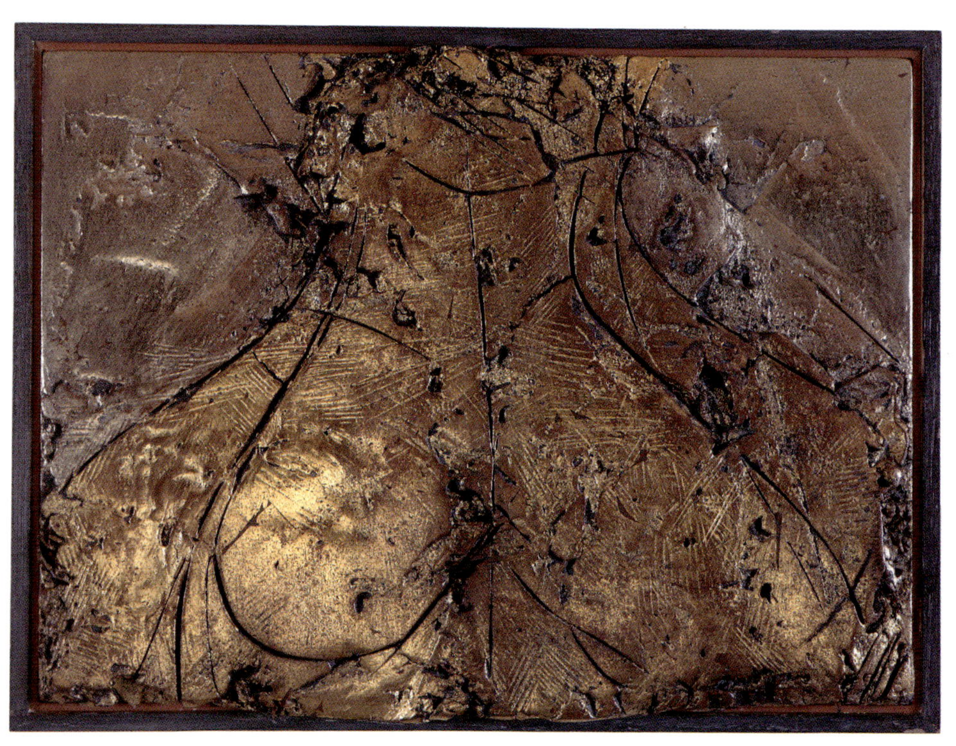

Frampold

1992
13 x $17\frac{1}{4}$ inches
24k moon gold over clay
Collection of Françoise B. Richardson

1996
$49^{1}/_{2}$ x 42 inches
23k gold over red, purple and black clay
Collection of Carol and Bill Deasy

Coin du Lestin XXIX

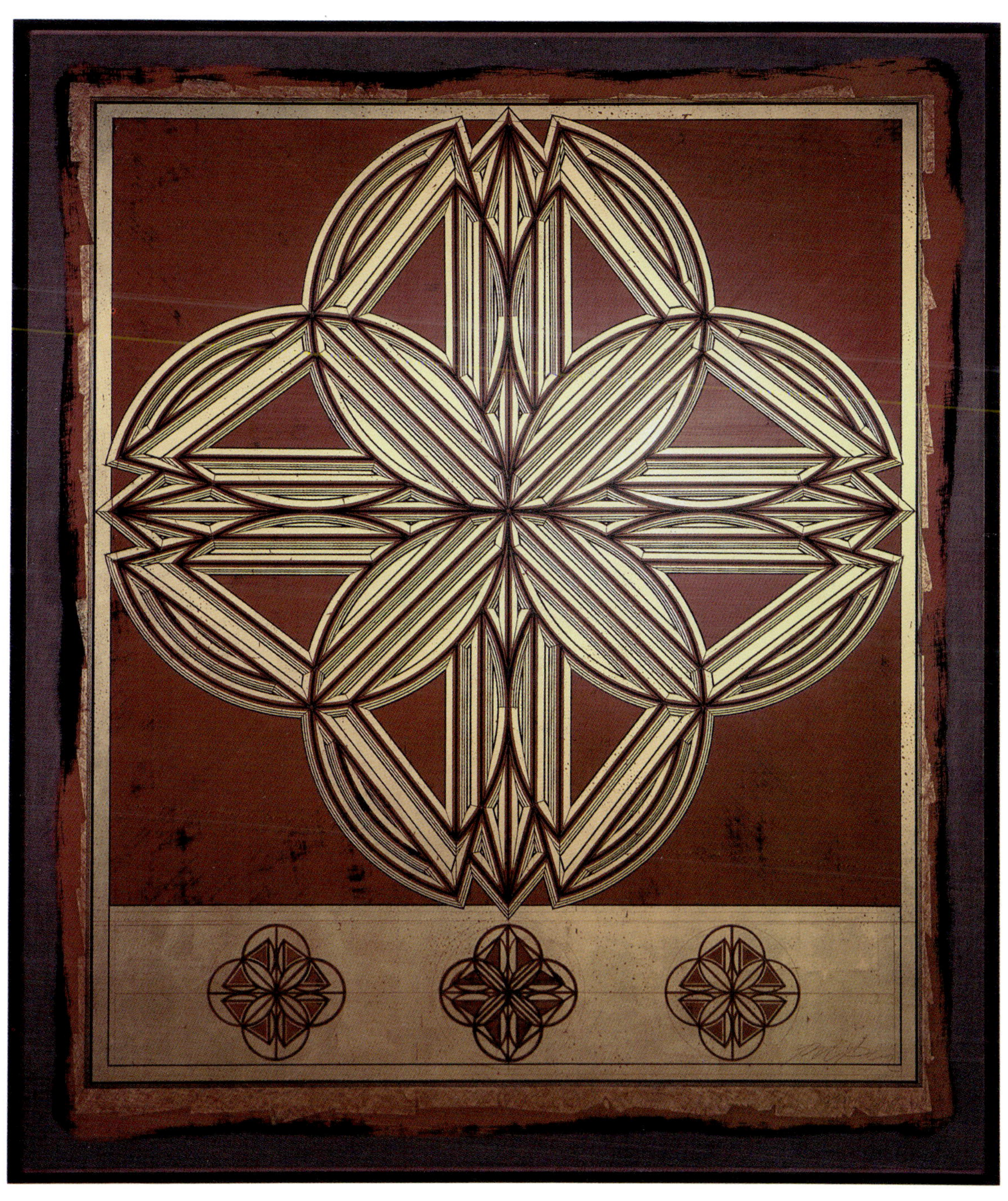

Diety

1995

87 x 78 inches

Sandblasted gold over clay and dental stone

Installation in the lobby of the Freeport-McMoRan Building, New Orleans, LA

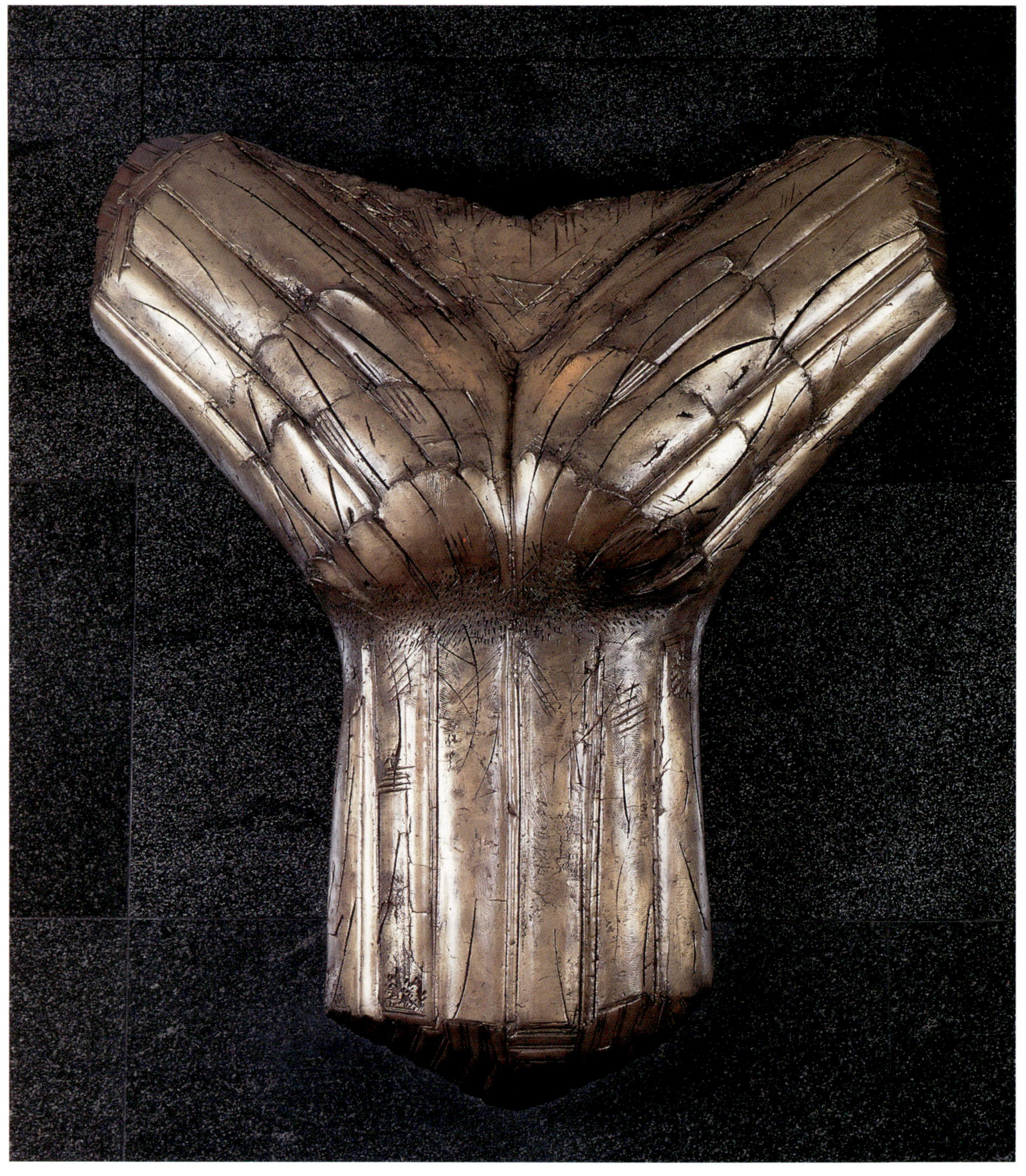

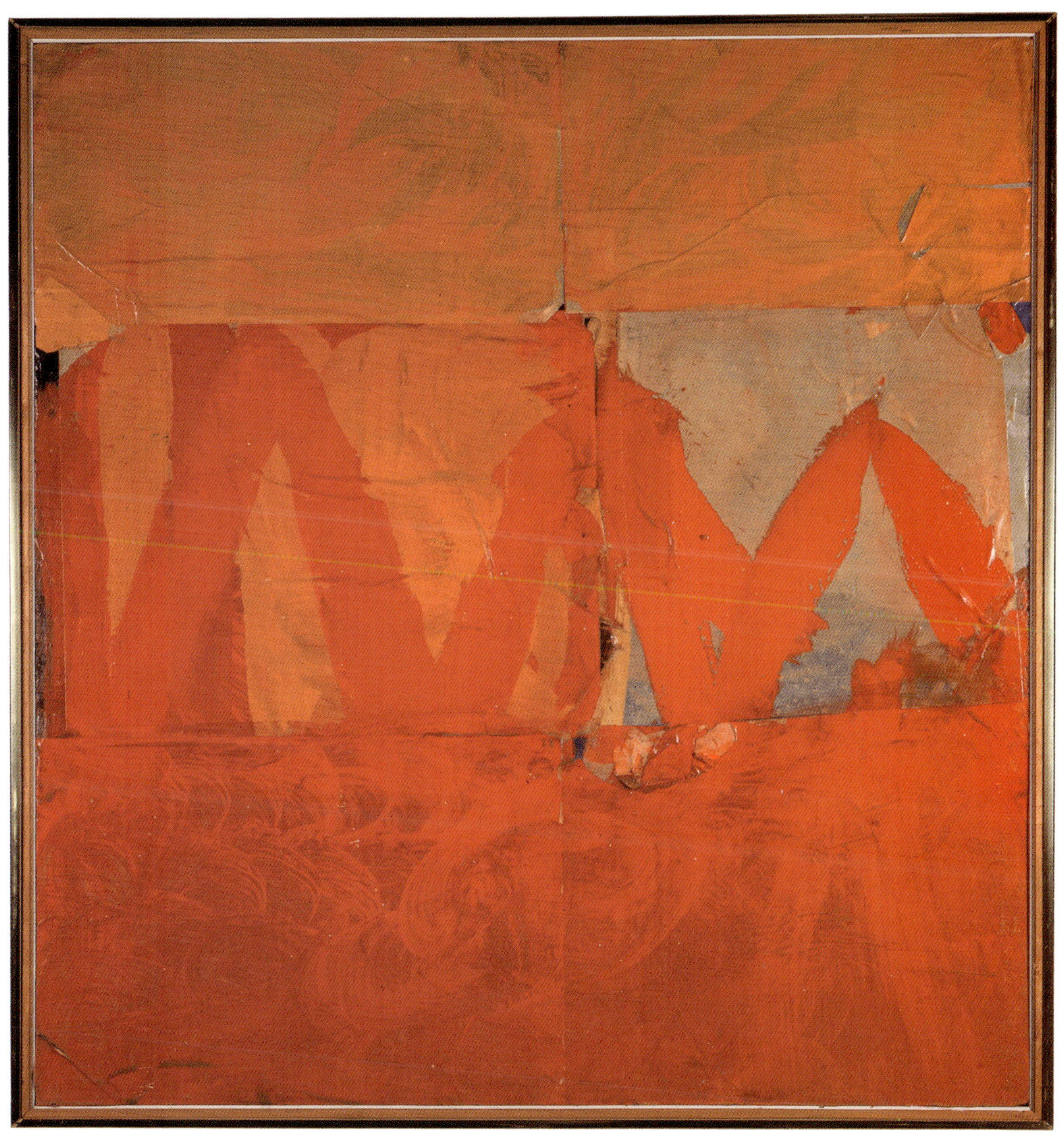

1959
50 x 47 inches
Acrylic and paper collage
Collection of the Artist

Red M

Flight

1992
7 x $19^{1}/_{2}$ inches
Clay over dental stone
Anonymous

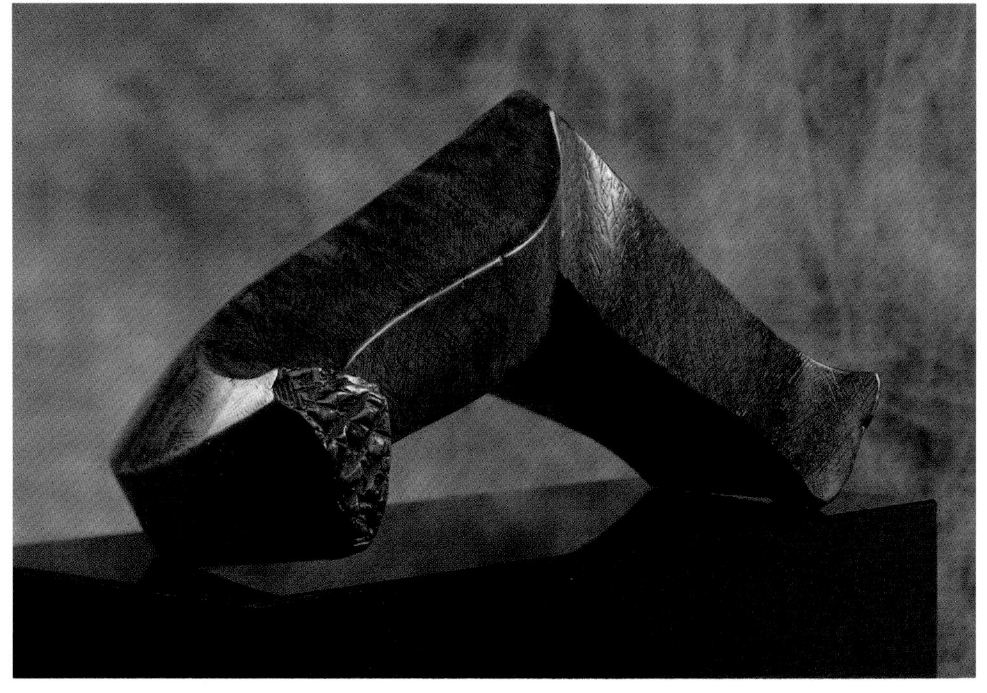

1995
55 x 49 1/4 inches
Gold over black and red clay
Collection of Mr. and Mrs. Robert J. Fabacher

Coin du Lestin XXIII

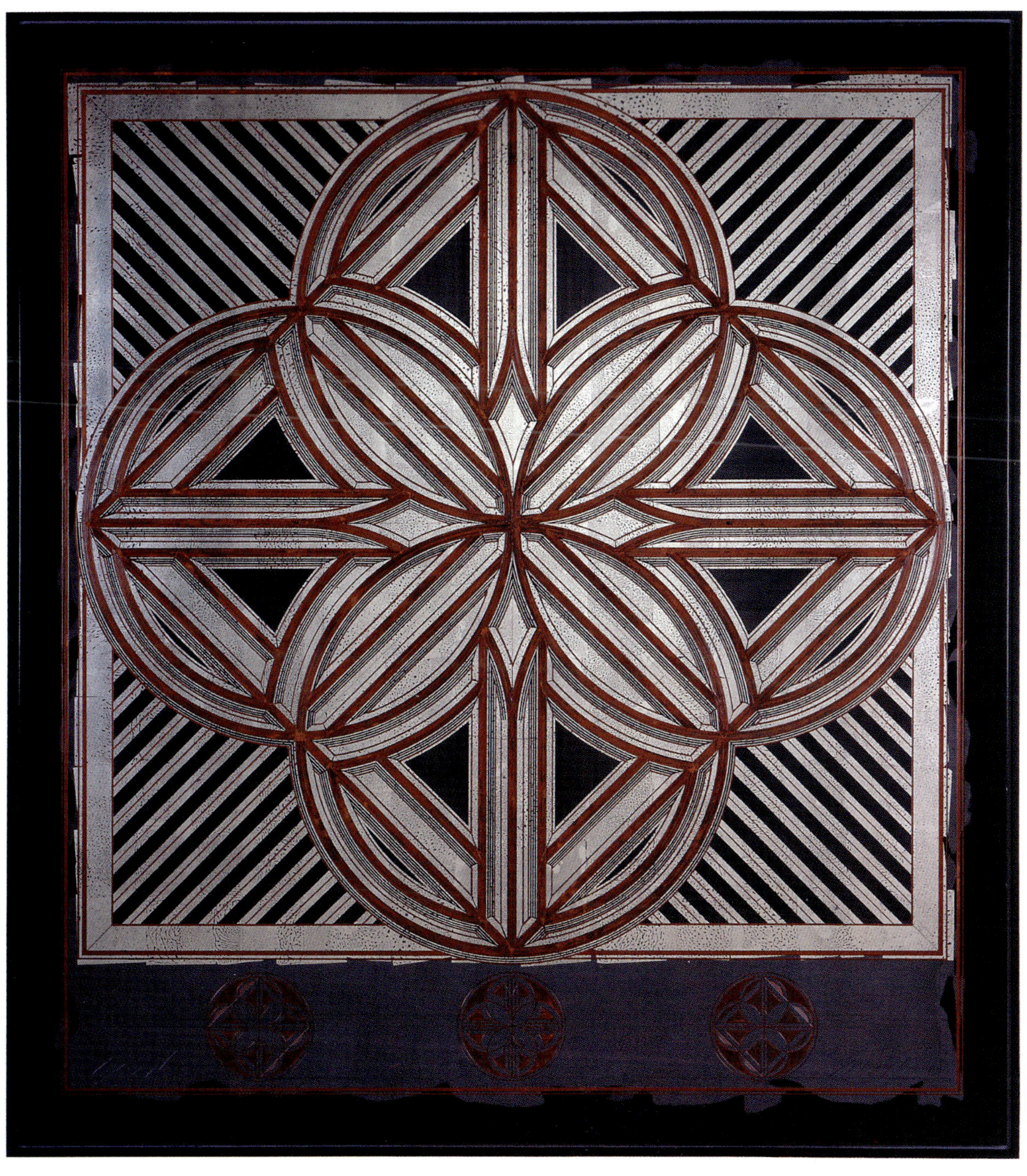

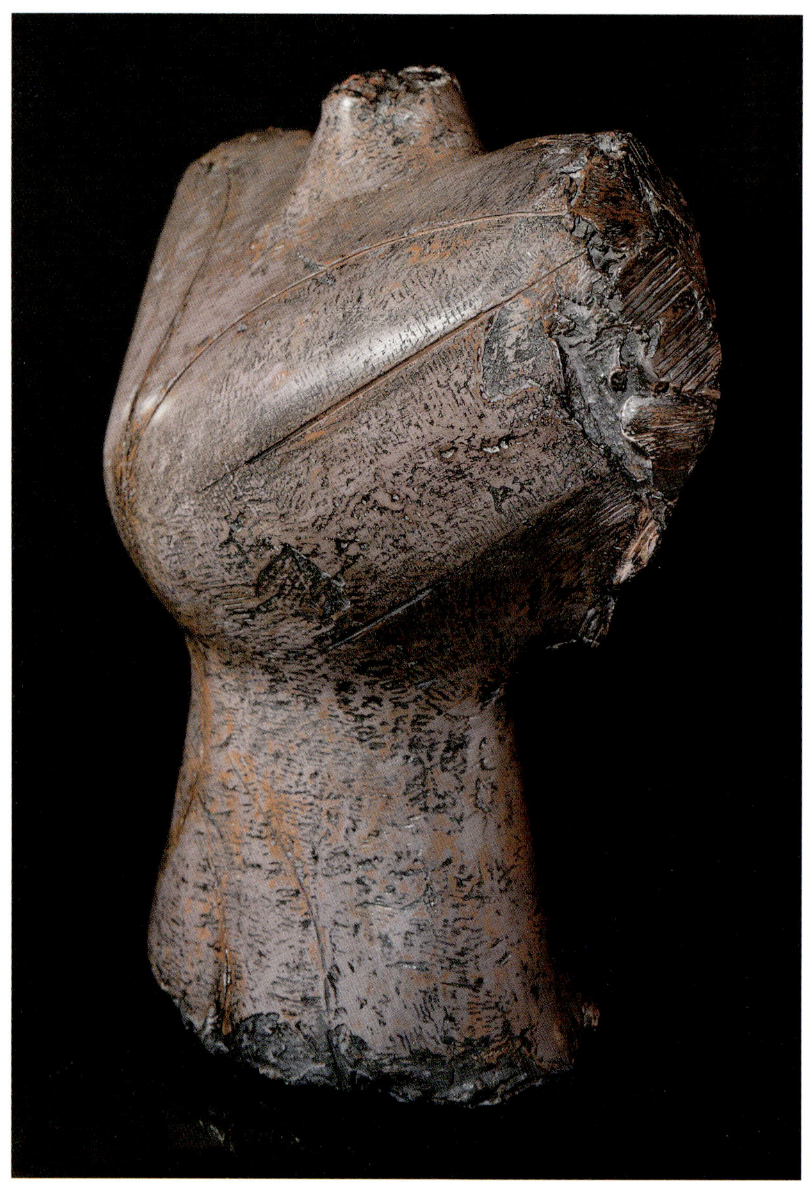

The Queen

1990
25 x 25 x 10 inches
Clay and dental stone
Collection of Mr. and Mrs. Joseph Canizaro

1994

55 x 49 1/4 inches

White gold over yellow, white and red clay

Collection of the Artist

Coin du Lestin XV

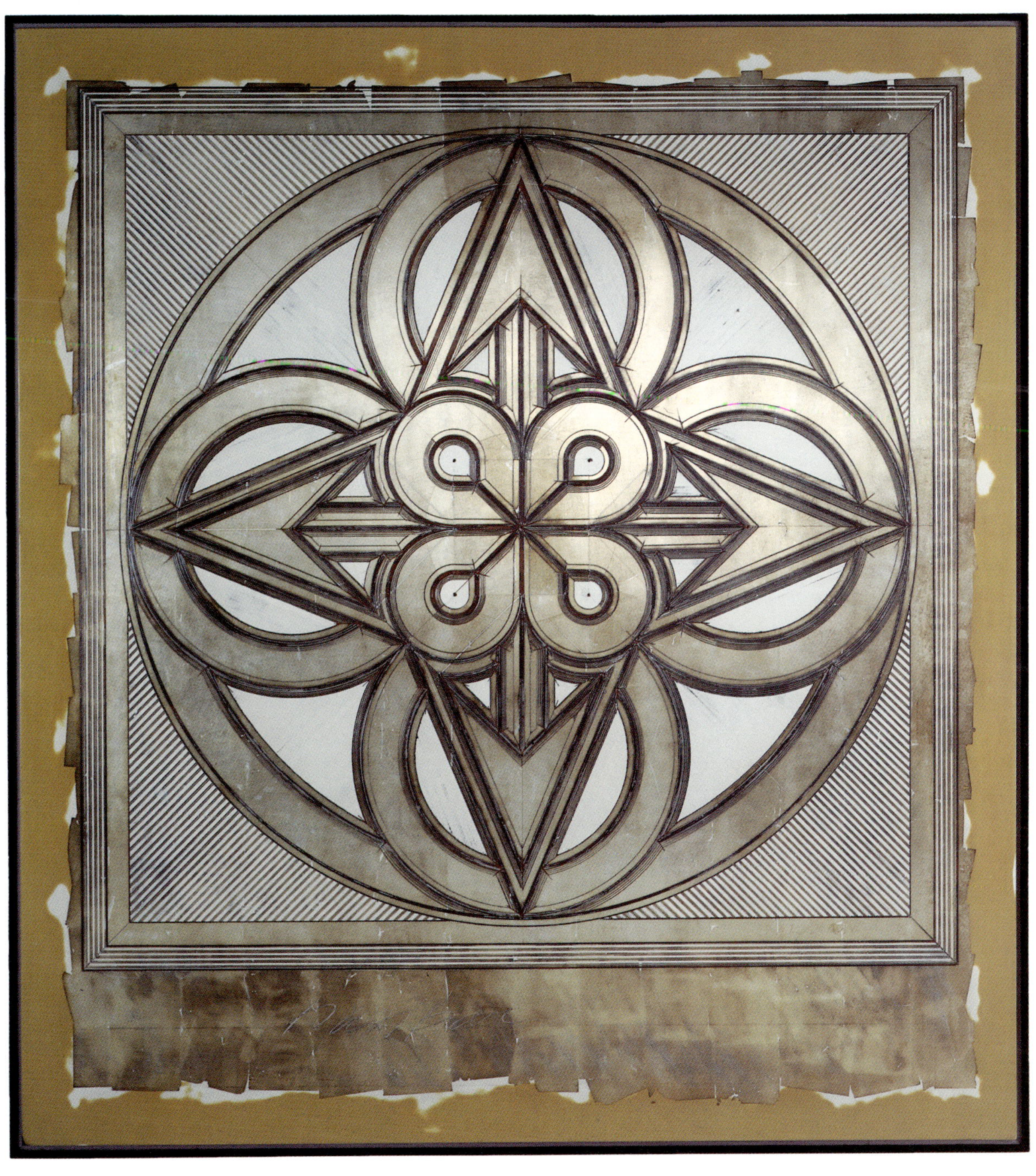

Untitled

1983
9 x 14 x 4 inches
Mixed media
Collection of the Artist

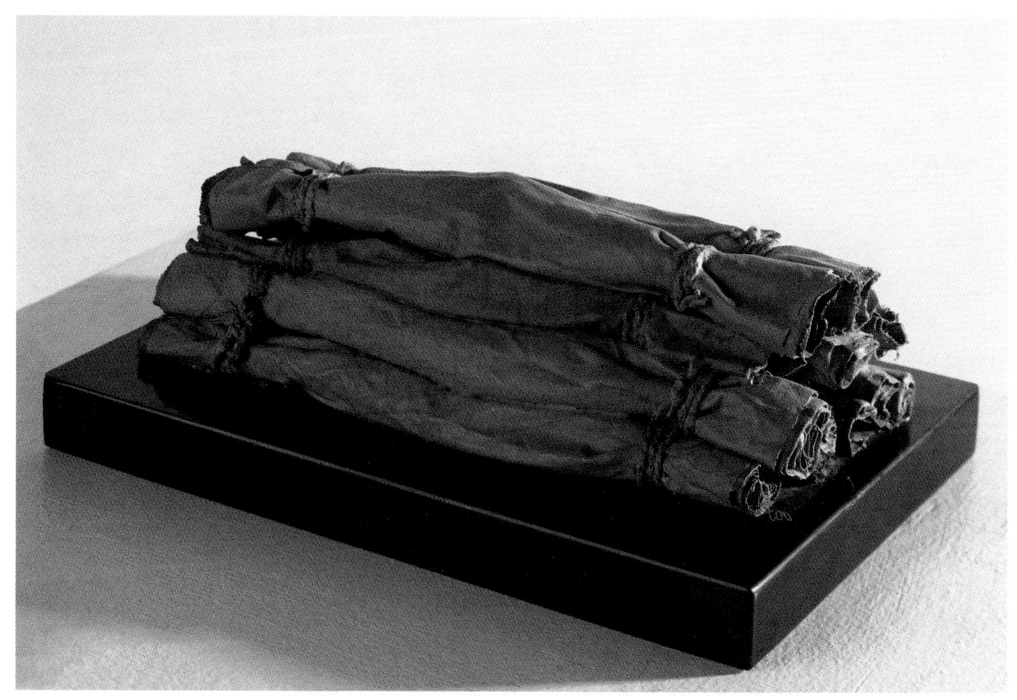

1967
23 x 24$^{3}/_{4}$ inches
Silver leaf over clay
Collection of Mr. and Mrs. William G. Richards

Untitled

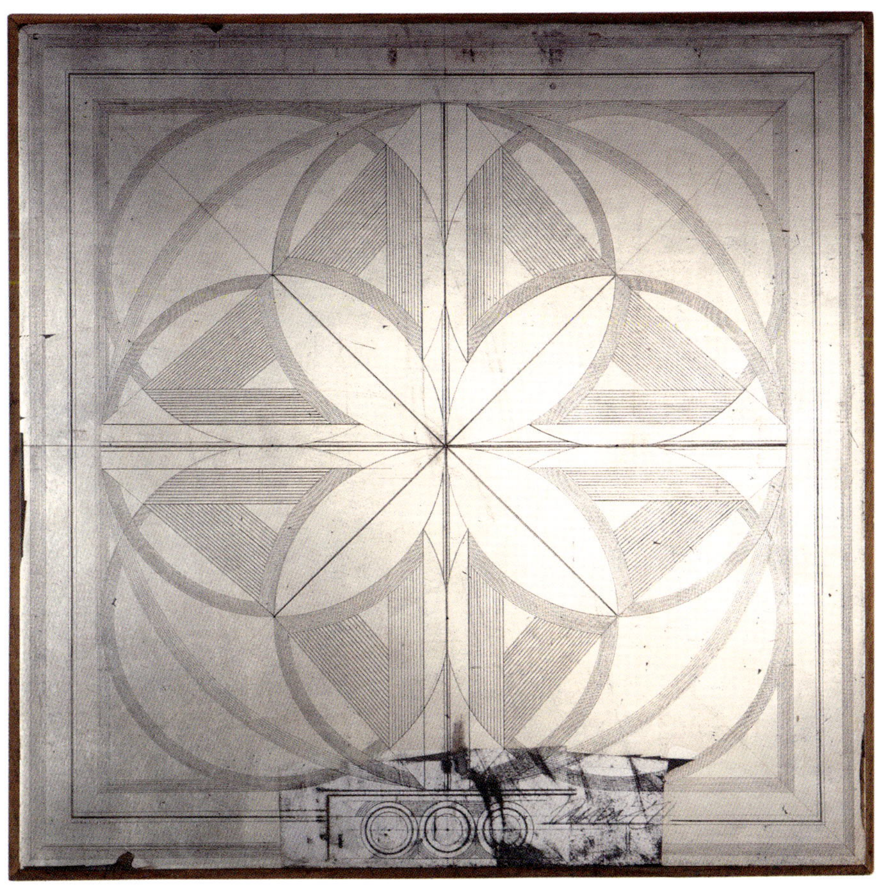

Coin du Lestin XXXIII

1997
$57^{1}/_{4}$ x $49^{3}/_{8}$ inches
Palladium leaf over red, blue and white clay
Collection of the Artist

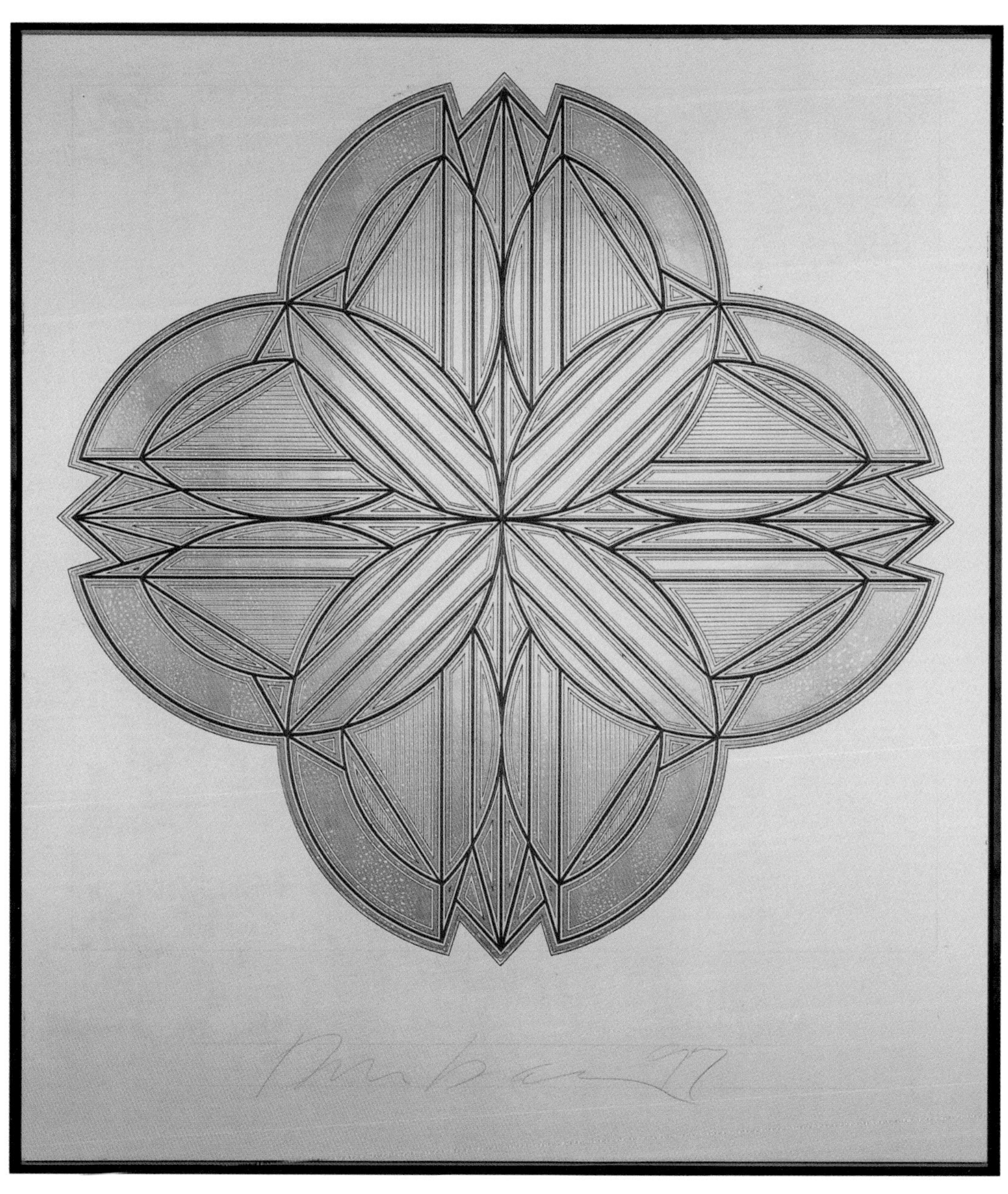

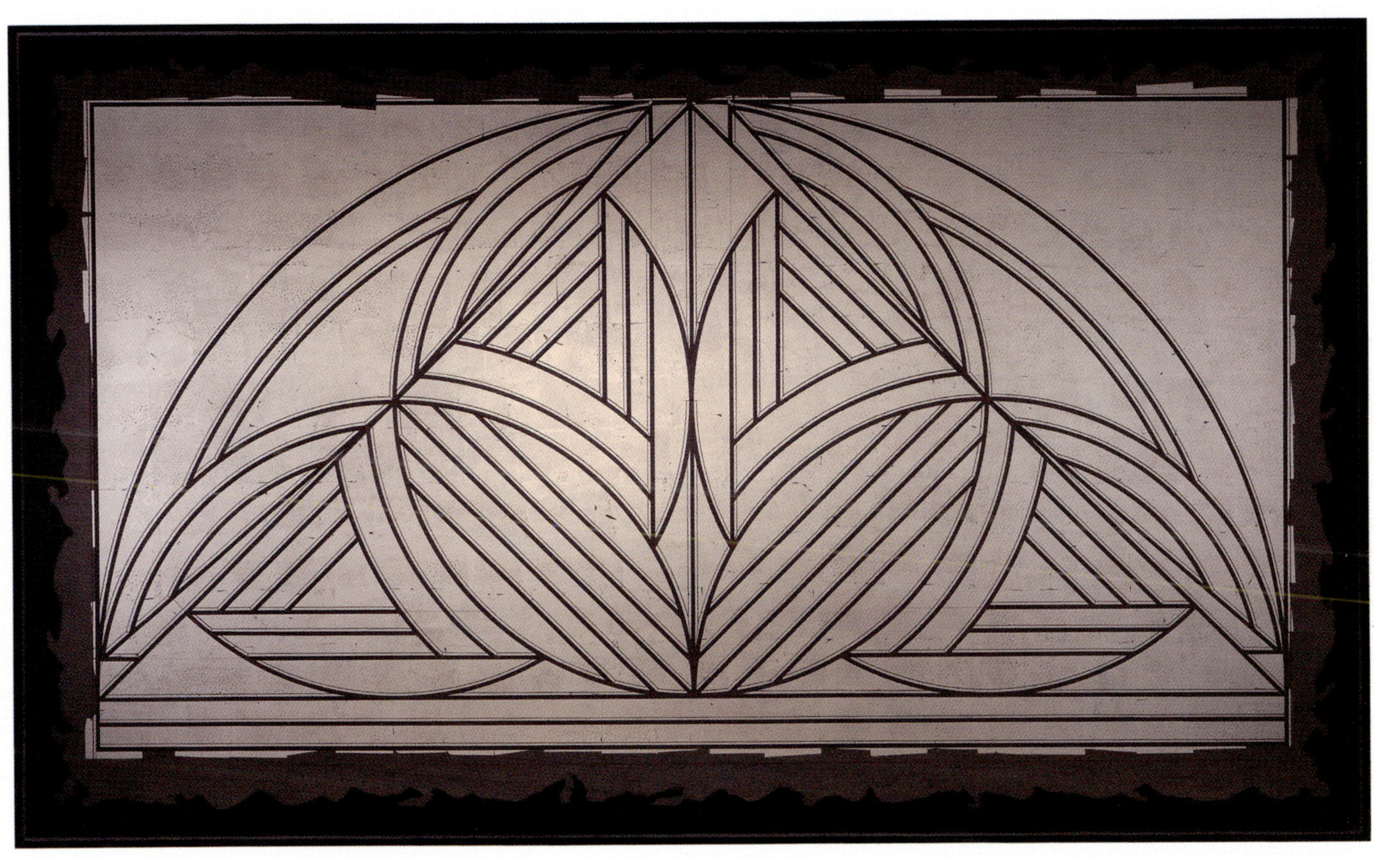

1995
$49^{1}/_{4} \times 81^{1}/_{2}$ inches
Palladium over red and black clay
Collection of the Tulane University
School of Law, New Orleans, LA

Untitled

Coin du Lestin XXIV

1996
43 x 43 inches
Palladium over blue, white and black clay
Collection of Biff and Barbara Motley

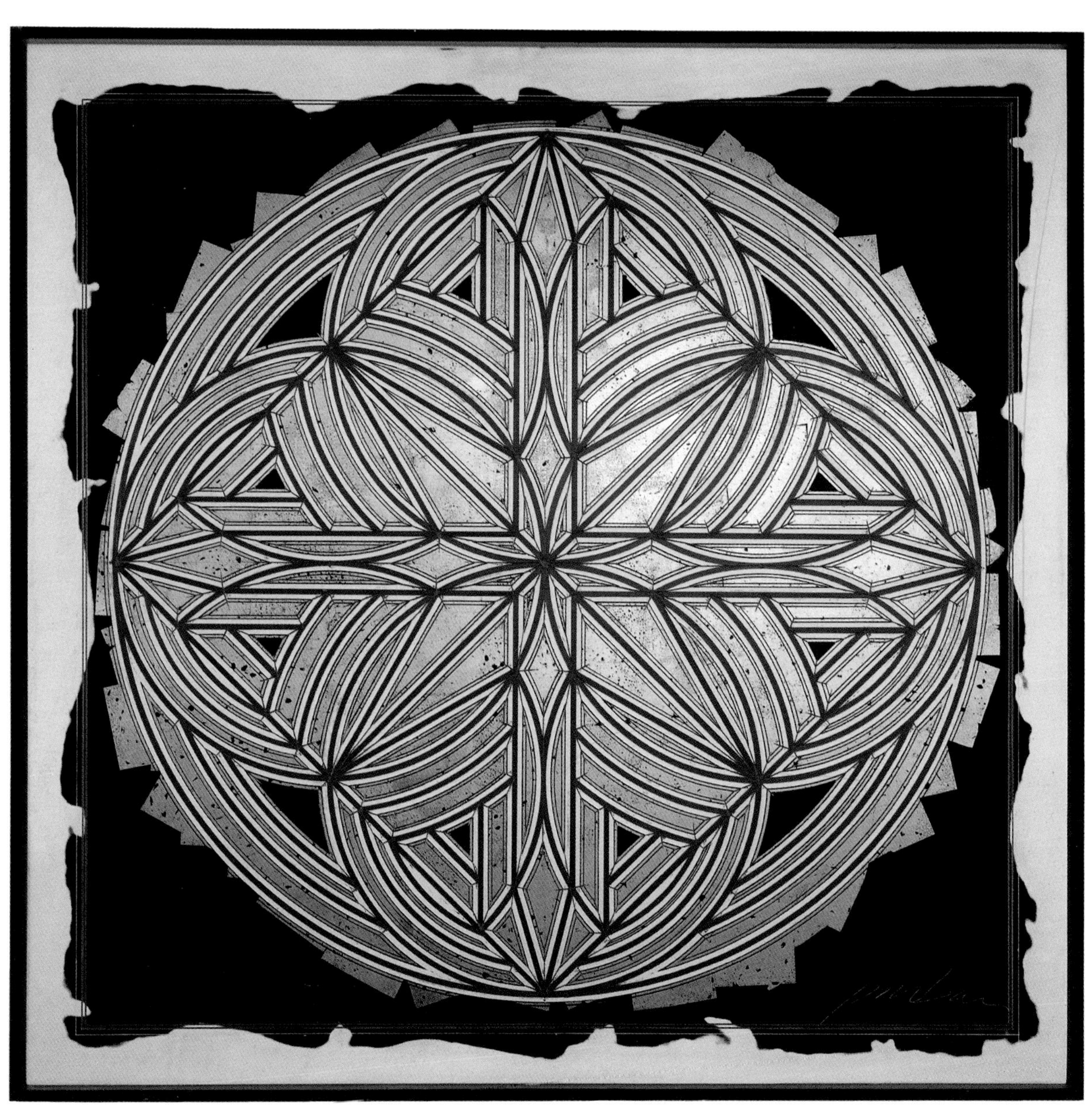

Untitled

1970
23 x 24¾ inches
White gold
Collection of the Artist

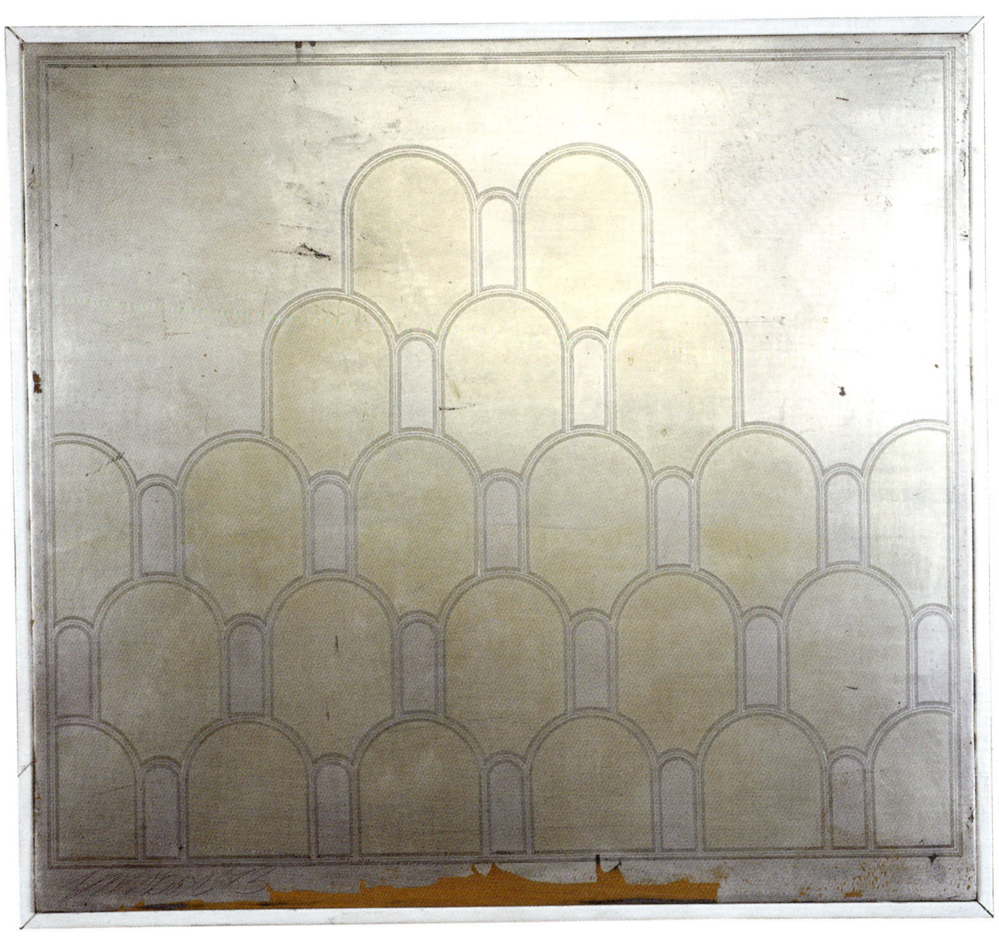

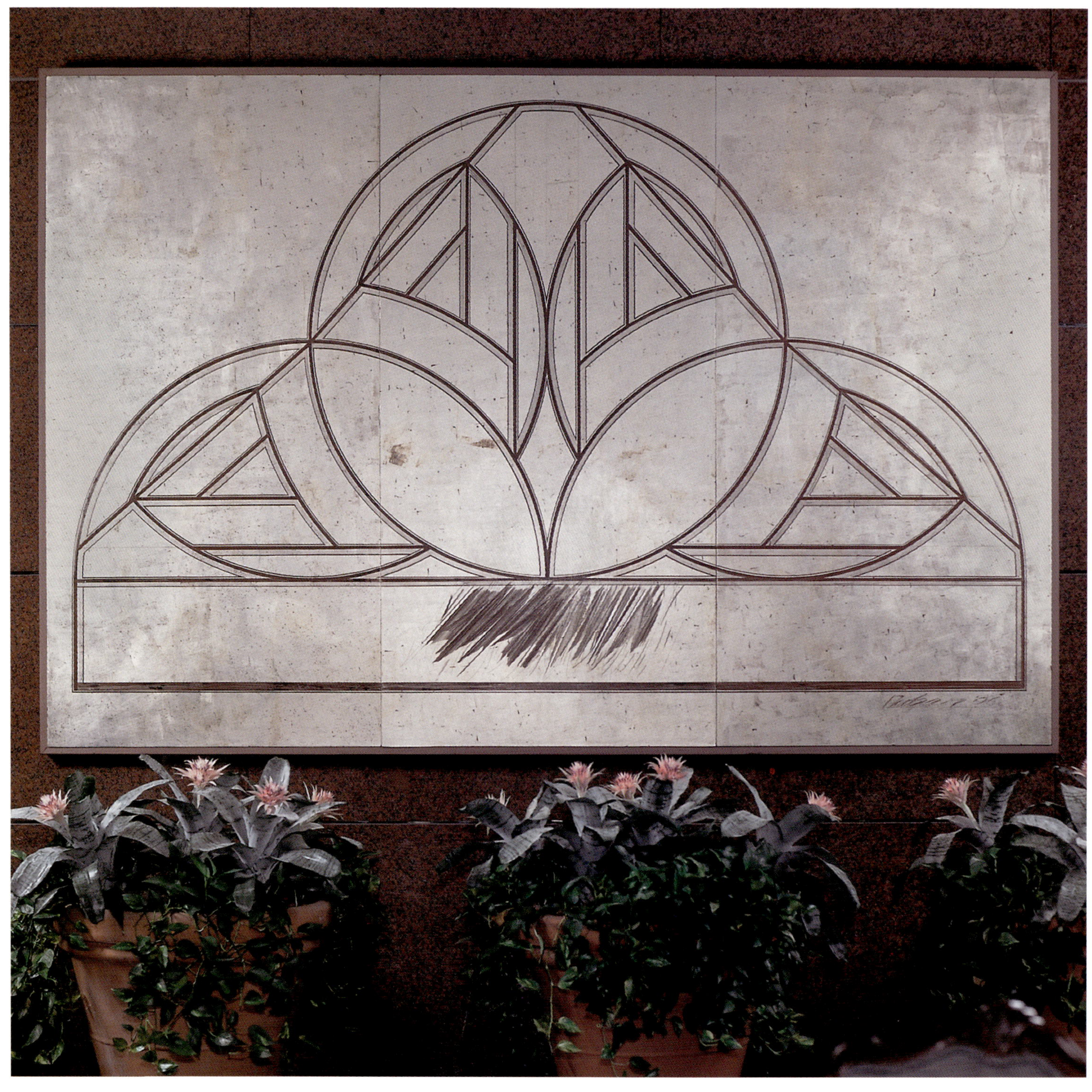

Coin du Lestin

1986
96 x 144 inches
Engraved silver leaf over clay
Installation in the lobby of the Texaco Building, New Orleans, LA

1988
49 1/2 x 62 inches
Egg emulsion
Anonymous

Las Gordas

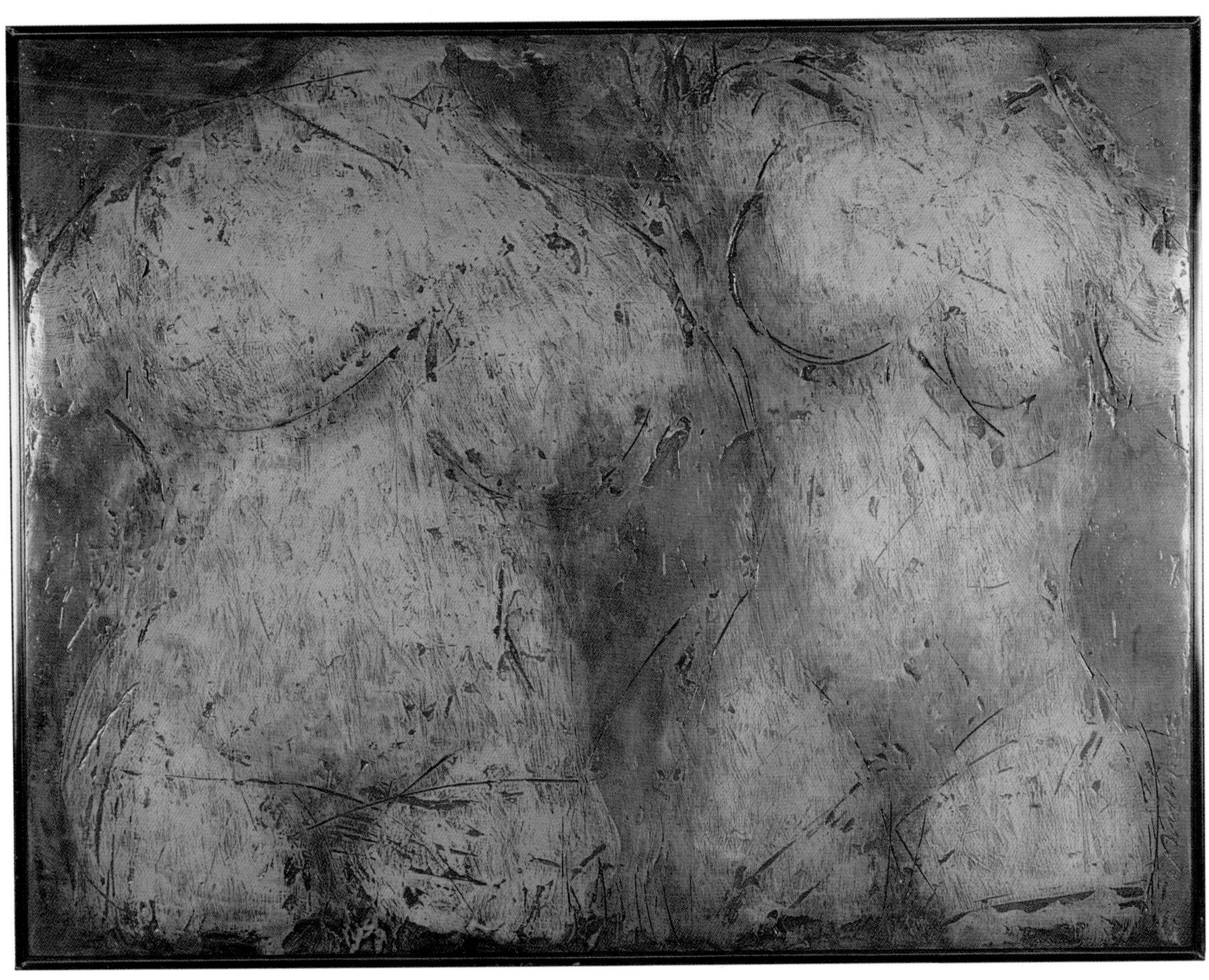

Coin du Lestin XXV

1996

$56\frac{1}{2}$ x 49 inches

Gold over clay

Collection of Dr. H. Russell Albright and Lee H. Ledbetter

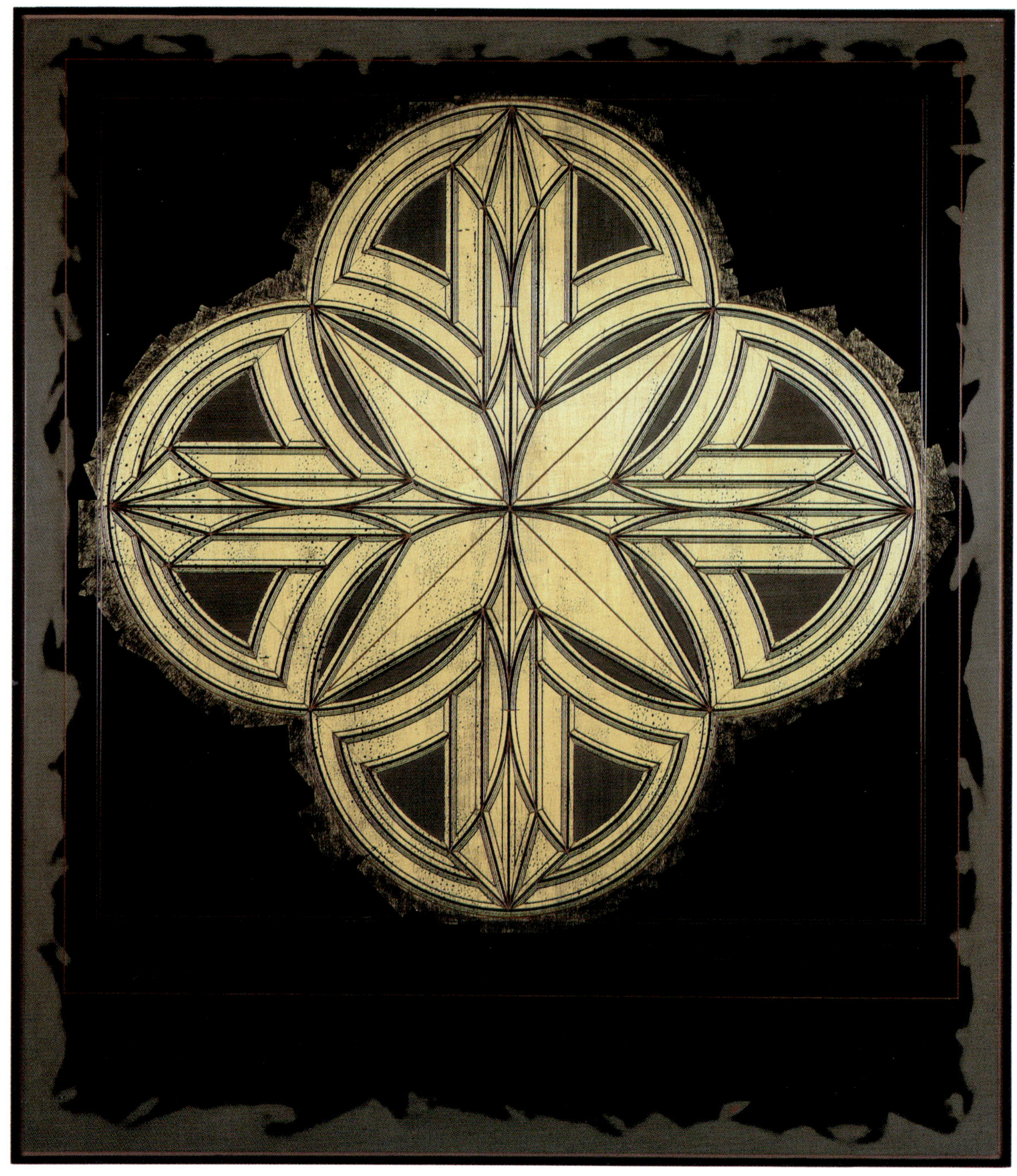

Loculus

1992
$35^3/_4 \times 49^1/_4$ inches
Gold over clay
Collection of Dr. and Mrs. John C. Bowen, III

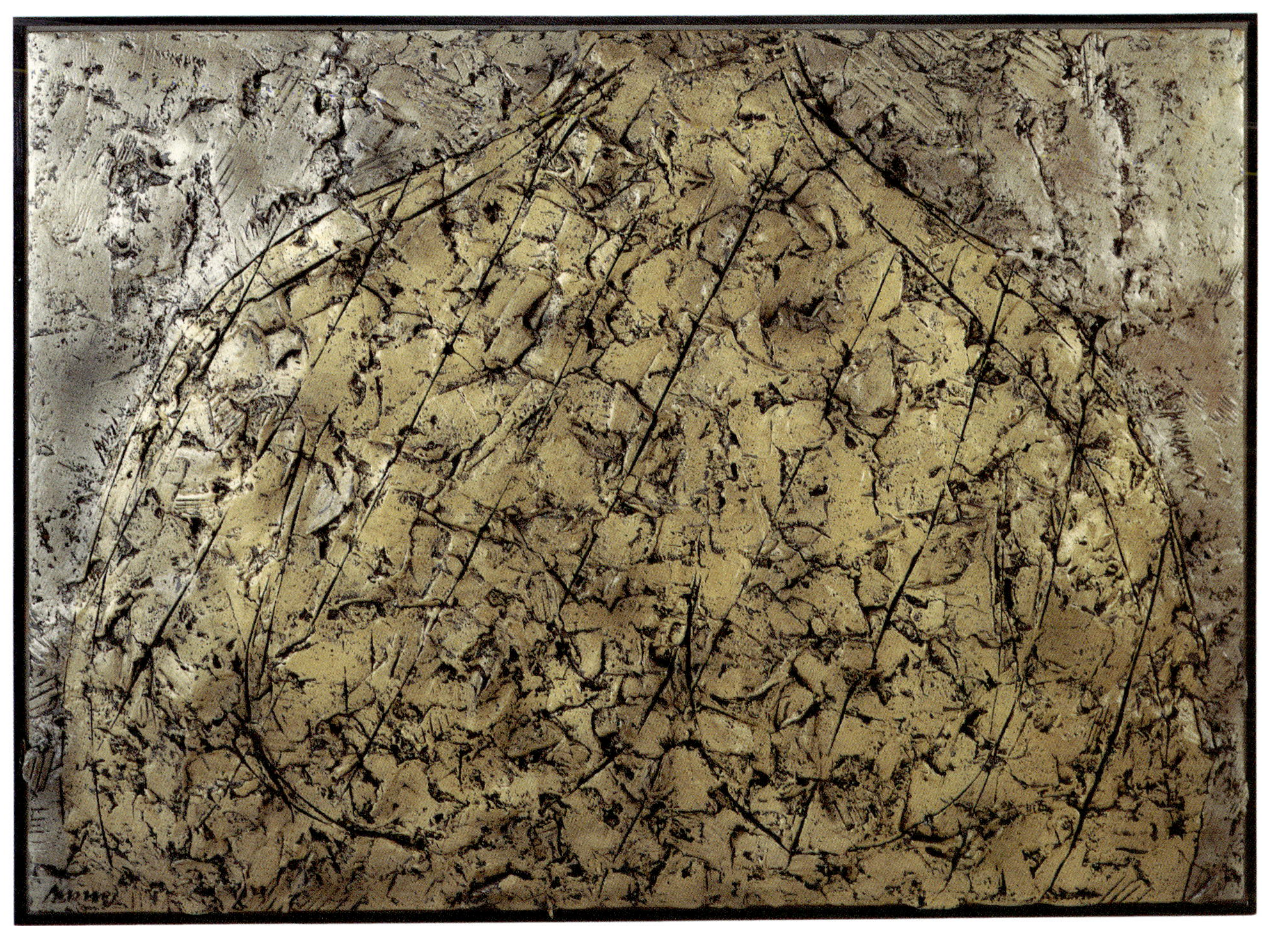

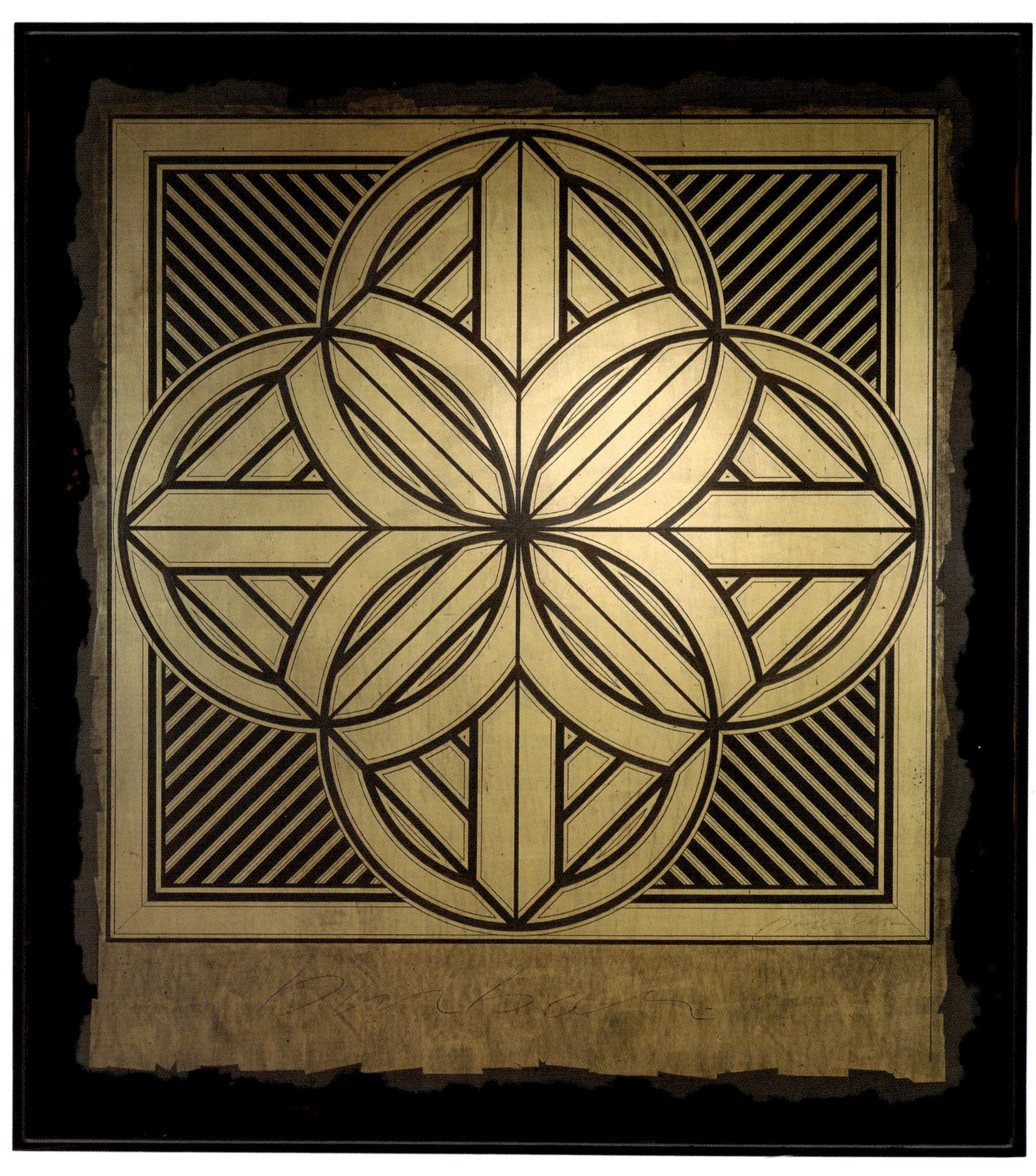

Coin du Lestin XIII

1994
55 x 48 3/8 inches
23k French gold over red, green and black clay
Collection of James A. Mounger

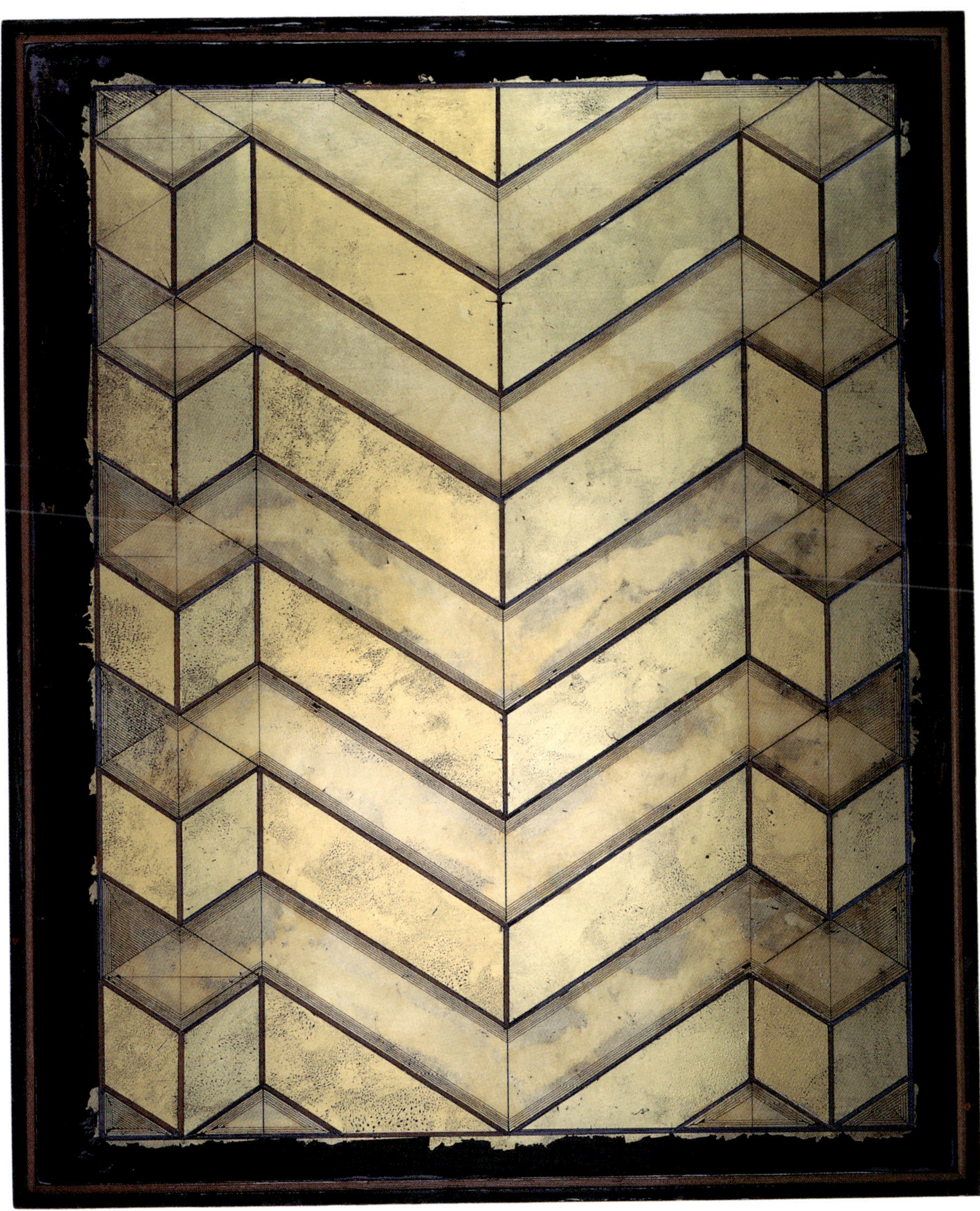

1990
$31^{1}/_{4}$ x $25^{1}/_{2}$ inches
Gold leaf over board and red, blue and black clay
Collection of Leon Irwin, III

Untitled

Coin du Lestin XXXIV

1997
$49^{1}/_{4}$ x $41^{1}/_{4}$ inches
$23^{1}/_{2}$k red gold leaf over
beige, black and purple clay
Anonymous

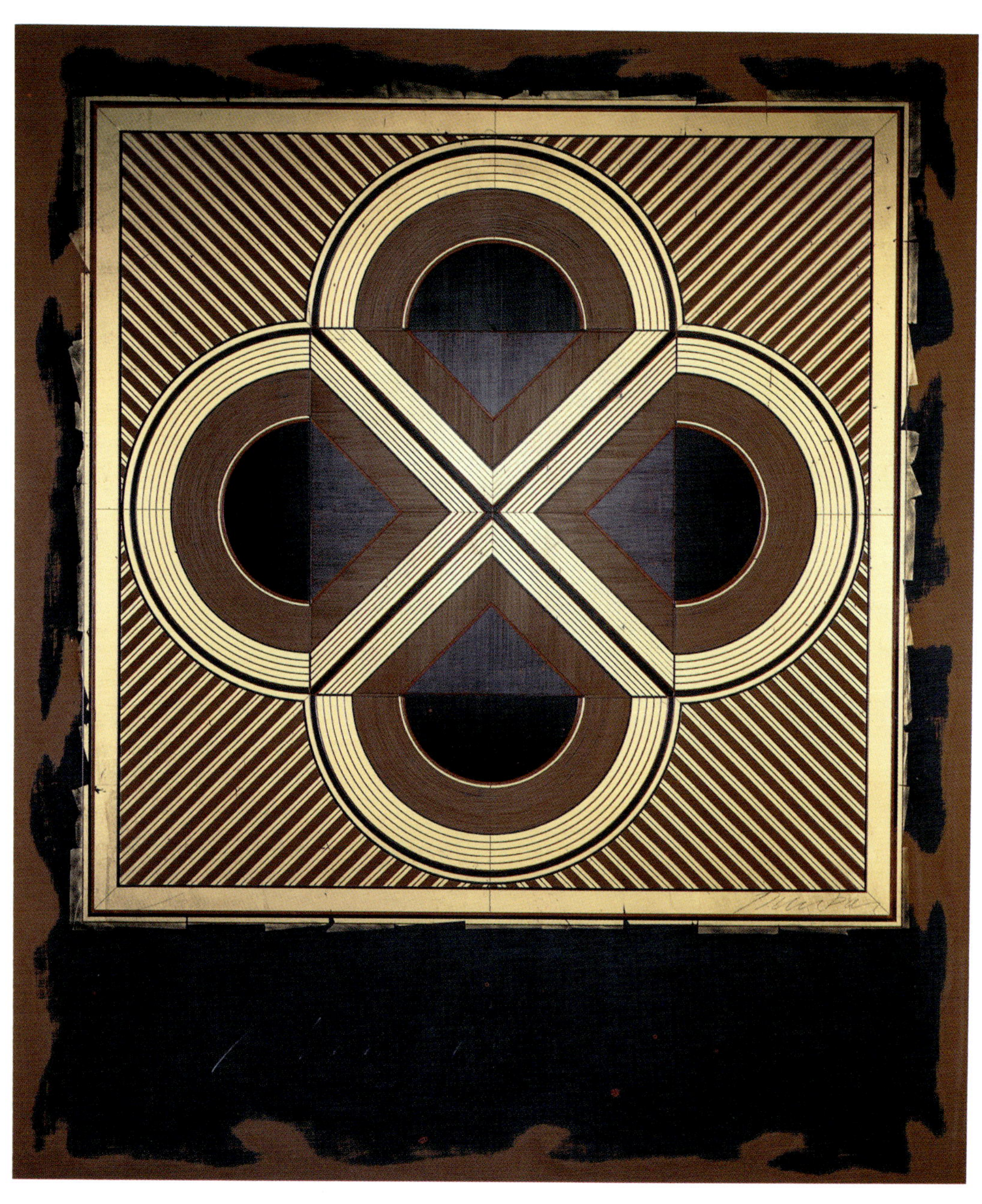

1987

80 x 123 inches

Mixed gold leaf karats over red and black clay

Installation in the lobby of the L,L&E Building, New Orleans, LA

Untitled

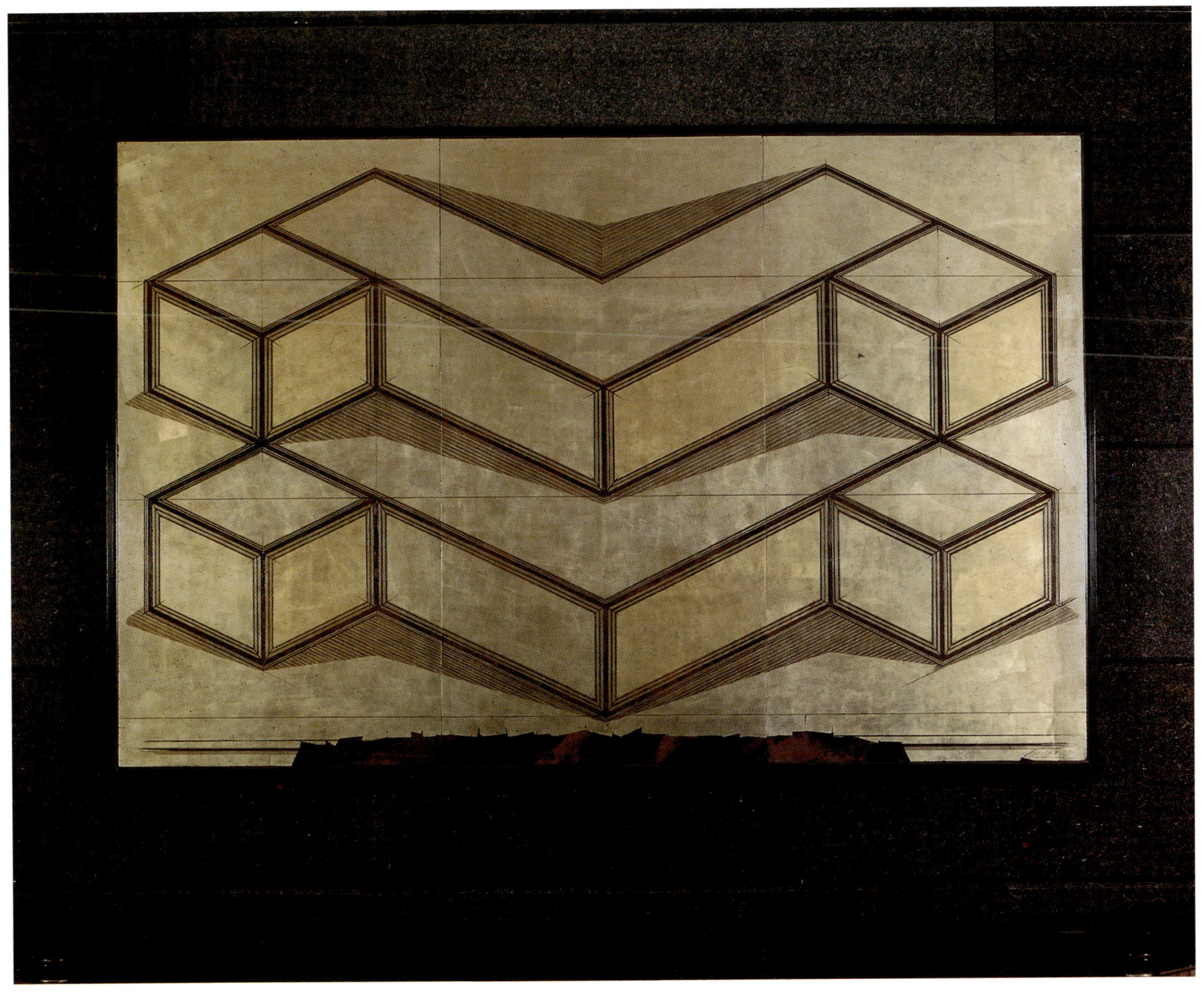

Untitled

1979
53 x 61 inches
Collage envelope
Collection of the Artist

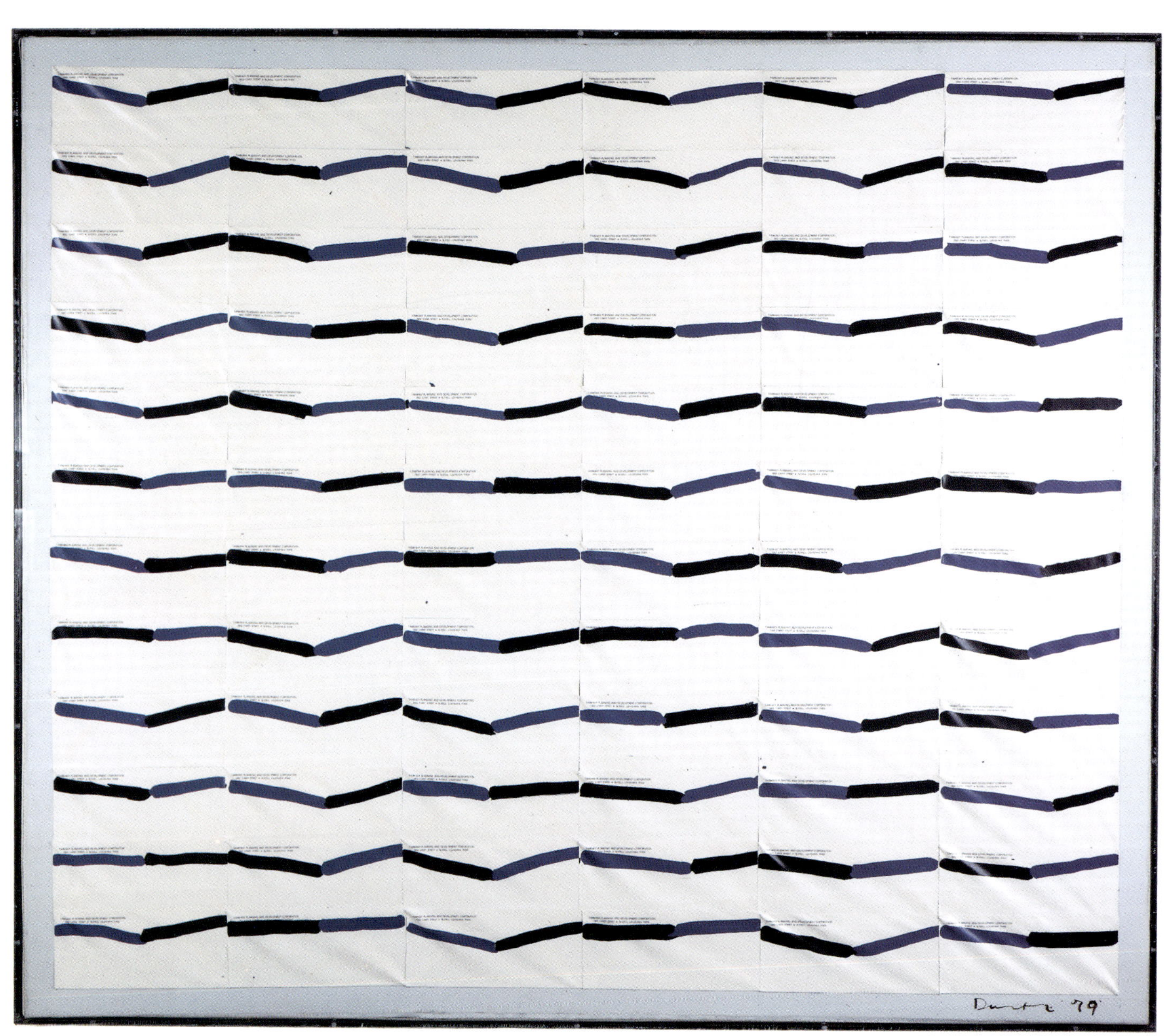

Coin du Lestin XXXVI

1997
$49^1/_4$ x $41^1/_4$ inches
Moon gold and palladium leaf
over beige, black and red clay
Anonymous

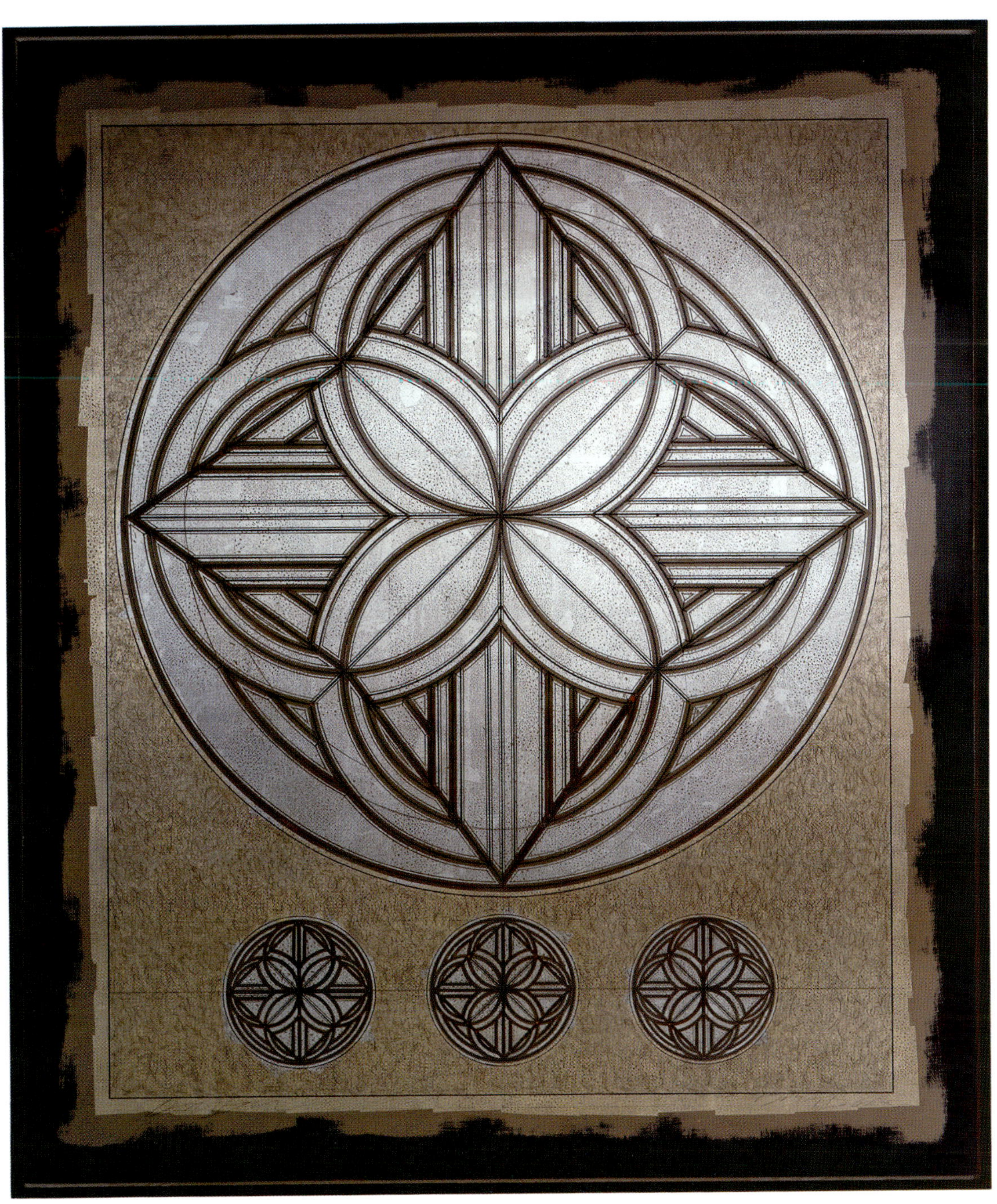

Untitled

1965
15 x 31 inches
Gold and silver leaf over clay
Anonymous

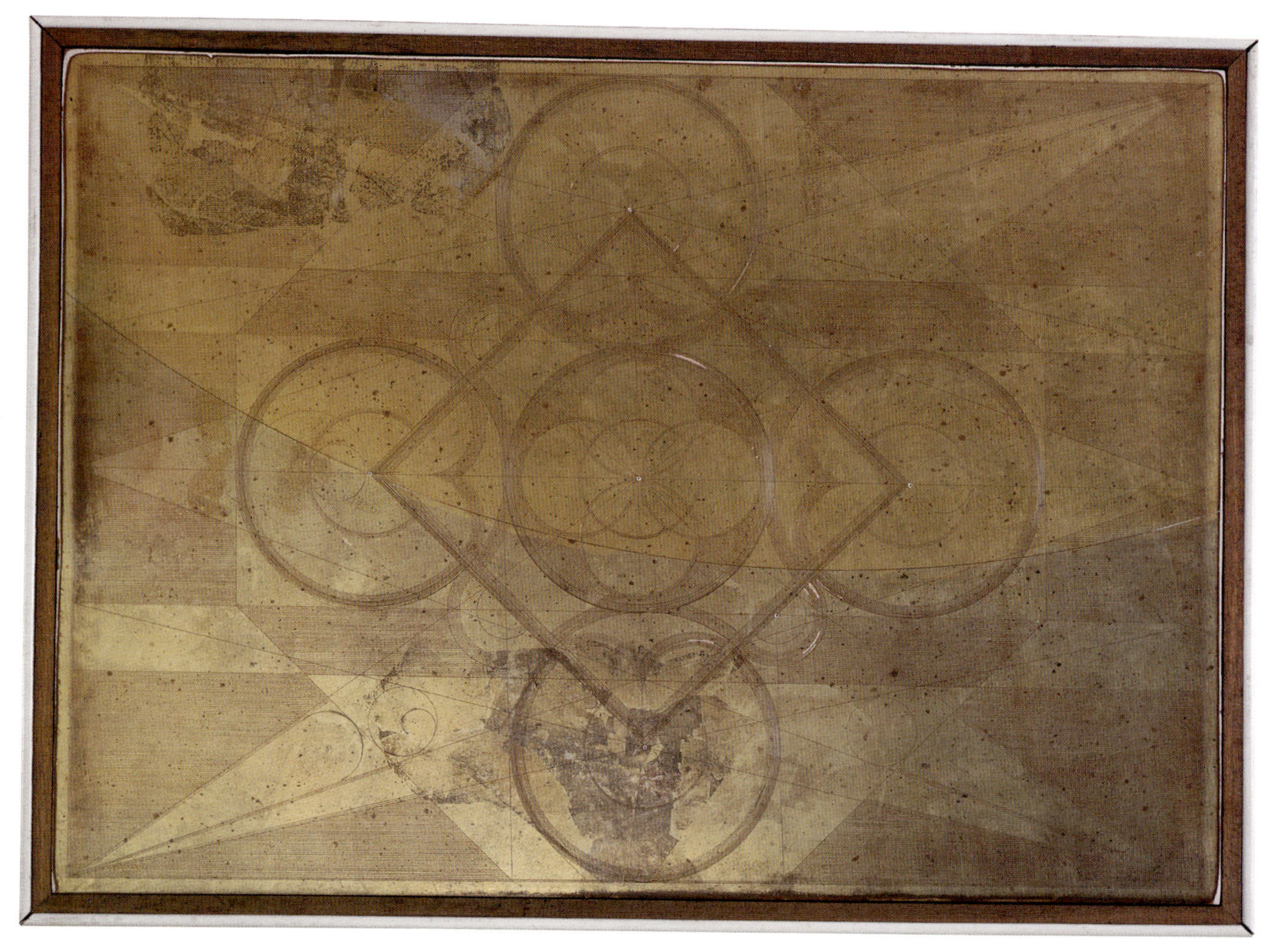